Great Places for Kids Parties (UK)

By Diane Mannion

Copyright Notice

Contents

Introduction

I still remember attending birthday parties when I was a kid, many eons ago; sandwiches, jelly and blancmange followed by a few games of pass the parcel and musical chairs. They would usually take place in somebody's house and we would compare gifts from the game of pass the parcel to see who got the best one.

One party in particular, that sticks in my mind, took place over the road from us. The houses on the other side of the road backed onto the 'red rec' and playground, and at the end of the party the parents opened the back door so that we could all go out to play. Although we were used to playing on the red rec, the fact that we were in a party somehow made it special and I remember proudly telling the other kids in the playground that we were in a party.

Today's kids are much more sophisticated and I dread to think what the reaction of my children and their friends would have been if I'd presented them with a dish of jelly marred by blancmange. Although I'm sure we enjoyed the parties of our day just as much as children do today, the trend is moving away from self-organised parties at home. Instead, there are numerous locations that host children's parties as well as others that will visit your home and take care of the entertainment for you.

Nowadays, children expect more too; in fact, the inclusion of a party bag is almost a pre-requisite. If you decide to forego the party bags you can guarantee that at least a couple of children will make it clear, in no uncertain terms, that they expect one. And heaven forbid that you should scrimp on the contents of the party bag – your reputation in the school yard depends on a good supply of small toys, novelties and sweets. Thankfully, a lot of the locations mentioned in this book include party bags so it saves you the bother of having to ensure that all the party bags have contents of equal value and that they are boy/girl appropriate. It is worth bearing in mind, though, that some locations charge extra for party bags as detailed under the relevant sections of the chapters.

I have included a great range of themed parties in this book to suit children with a broad range of interests. Where possible I have chosen the type of parties that are widely available throughout the UK. Each chapter has a case study so that you can get an idea of what a typical party with that theme entails. Many of the organisations that I have included as case studies are major companies with branches up and down the country. Where I haven't been able to find UK wide organisations for particular themes, I have instead included case studies that are typical of the types of parties that are run by various companies in different parts of the country.

Although many of the organisations featured in this book have children's birthday party packages, you may decide to throw a children's party for another reason. Perhaps you and a group of friends want a novel way to celebrate Christmas or Easter with your children. You might have a parent and toddler group, playgroup, or post-natal group that has an annual anniversary party. If you want to make your anniversary party a little special then you may prefer to host it at another premises rather than at your usual meeting place. What about organising a goodbye party if your children are leaving nursery and moving on to school?

There could be all sorts of reasons for children's parties so, although this book generally features birthday parties, it is worth bearing in mind that you could find lots of exciting ideas for other types of celebrations too. Even if you choose to host your party with one of the featured organisations that has set birthday party packages, I am sure that the majority of organisations would have no problem adapting the party to suit other celebrations. You will also find that I have referred to 'parents' throughout the book for simplicity. However, this also refers to guardians, carers or other people organising parties on behalf of children.

Because the parties featured in this book are so diverse, there will be different requirements for each. It is therefore important to make sure that the children are dressed appropriately for the type of party they are attending. Another important point is that most organisations that host parties will need to know if any of the children have medical conditions, special needs or special dietary requirements. Where the individual organisations have asked for this information, I have stated it in the relevant chapter.

How this Book is Organised

Each of the chapters is based on a theme, which is, for the main part, location based i.e. you have to go to the organisers that host that particular type of party. However, there are some parties where the organisers come to you. The overview at the start of each chapter briefly explains what is involved for each kind of party. I have then included a case study for each chapter, which features an organisation that provides that type of party. You will also find lots of colourful pictures to enable you to browse through the chapters with your children.

The case study is split into detailed sections so that all the information you need is at hand. For example, you can find out what type of preparation you need to make, how much it is likely to cost, what is included in the cost, what age group the party is aimed at and how many children you can invite. I have also included any additional details that you may want to know.

You will find that some chapters are more detailed than others and there are two reasons for this. The first reason is that I have relied on information available from the organisations concerned and some have provided more information than others. Secondly, some organisations offer a range of different party packages for you to choose from. However, I have followed the same format for the case study sections to enable you to compare information quickly and easily.

Organised parties can be expensive, which is why I've included a cost section in each of the case studies. This will give you an idea of what you can expect to pay. When thinking about cost it is important to think about not just the standard cost of the party, but also what is included in that cost. Each of the case studies includes a 'What's Included?' section as well as a 'Cost' section. These two sections give information about any extras that have to be paid for. I have also included details of special offers that are available for some of the parties.

One final note is that the information contained in each of these case studies is correct at the time of compilation but you should bear in mind that this information is subject to change. Therefore, neither I nor the named organisations can guarantee that the information presented will remain the same.

Acknowledgements

I would like to thank the many organisations featured in this book for their co-operation and enthusiasm. A number of these organisations have provided valuable feedback and updates, which have helped me to ensure that the content is as accurate and current as possible. My special thanks go to those organisations that also agreed to include a special offer exclusive to people buying this book.

A big thank you goes to my fellow authors who have been a great source of support and have helped me with my many questions surrounding the book publishing and marketing process. Being an Independent author requires a lot of input relating to, not only writing, but the whole process involving formatting, publication, promotion and marketing. Thankfully, there is a great support network amongst the Independent author community. The help and advice of my fellow authors has been invaluable in enabling me to bring this book to market. There are too many names to list amongst the Independent authors that help to promote the work of others, but I would especially like to thank the following people:

- Alice Huskisson who has provided useful help and support in so many ways and has become a valued friend.

- Joanne Phillips for sharing useful advice regarding printing options as well as tips on book marketing.

- Charlie Plunkett, a fellow parenting author, for sharing her knowledge of the marketing options for parenting books.

- Terry Tyler for help and advice relating to book promotion.

- Guy Portman for his continued support and interest in my work.

- Clare Davidson, Rachel Dove and Anne Coates for wonderful reviews of my first book, "Kids' Clubs and Organisations", and their ongoing support.

Thanks also to Derek Arthur for sharing ideas and suggestions.

Last but not least I would also like to thank my husband for his unwavering support and encouragement.

Chapter 1: Have them Turning Somersaults

Gymnastics Parties

OVERVIEW

Gymnastics parties can be great fun for kids and can introduce them to apparatus that they may not have a chance to try out at school. This is because centres that are specifically for gymnastics training usually have a wider range of gymnastics equipment than schools. An example of this is the City of Manchester Institute of Gymnastics (CMIG), which is featured in our case study. This venue, in particular, trains young people up to Olympic standard so the selection of apparatus is comprehensive.

Apart from getting enjoyment from the party, children might discover a love of gymnastics and want to attend regular classes. This is no bad thing since gymnastics can teach children a wide variety of skills in terms of physical development, social aspects, commitment and self-discipline.

There are many centres throughout the UK offering gymnastics parties and the venue covered in our case study is just one example. The focus for CMIG is on its high quality gymnastics facilities and, although it does not have facilities for party food on the premises, many other venues do.

With CMIG it is important to note that party food facilities are available close to the party venue.

When looking for venues offering gymnastics parties, you may find it easier to search for one in your area that is part of a multi-sports facility. These can often be local authority controlled but you may also find gymnastics centres in the private sector. To find a private gymnastics centre near you that holds children's birthday parties, try entering, 'gymnastics centre + children's birthday parties (*your area*)' into an Internet search engine. Once you have found a suitable centre within easy reach, the following case study should give you a general idea of what to expect. You can then compare the case study to the birthday parties organised by your local gymnastics centre and ask appropriate questions about what is on offer.

CASE STUDY

City of Manchester Institute of Gymnastics:
http://www.cityofmanchestergymnastics.co.uk/.
Email: info@cityofmanchestergymnastics.co.uk.
Phone: 0161 223 5705.

The Location

City of Manchester Institute of Gymnastics, Garratt Way, Gorton, Manchester, M18 8HE. N.B. There is a location map on the contacts page of the website.

Preparation

Parents and carers can pick up a booking form from the reception area at the Institute of Gymnastics. There is no time limit for booking parties but, as with all types of parties, you will stand a better chance of your chosen date being available if you book sooner rather than later. As the venue does not provide invitations, you will have to purchase your own.

The Party

Children have a one hour session in a well-equipped gym, which is available exclusively to them for the duration of the session. They take part in games connected to gymnastics using the trampoline, trampettes, springboards and vaults. During their time in the gym they are supervised by John Smethurst who is a fully qualified coach as well as a double Commonwealth Gold and Bronze medallist.

There are specific times allocated to birthday parties, which are:

Saturday 1.30 – 2.30pm; and,
Sunday 12.30 – 1.30pm.

Suitable Ages

The Manchester Institute of Gymnastics children's parties are suitable for children from the ages of 4 upwards.

Food

The Institute of Gymnastics does not provide food and parents cannot bring party food onto the premises. However, there are several local fast food restaurants including KFC and McDonald's so it is possible to have a multi-venue party. The Institute of Gymnastics also has an arrangement with Sivori's café, which is opposite the venue. Sivori's will rope off an area of the café specifically for children from the gymnastics centre, and it offers a children's menu.

How many Children?

The parties are for a maximum of 20 children.

Cost

The charge for birthday parties is a flat fee of £100.00. A non-refundable deposit of £50.00 is payable in advance, with the balance due on the day of the party.

What's Included?

The charge includes use of the equipment, and taking part in gymnastics related games supervised by a qualified coach. Although there are no facilities for party food on the premises, parents can bring in a birthday cake and party bags.

Points to Consider

All children attending the party must wear appropriate clothing such as a tracksuit, leotard or shorts and t-shirt. For safety reasons all long hair has to be tied back and all jewellery removed. The venue's rules state that they reserve the right to refuse admission to the party for any child who is not suitably dressed.

Chapter 2: Make a Swim for It

Swimming Parties

OVERVIEW

Most children love swimming. That's understandable because, apart from being good for you, it's a really fun activity. Of course, if you gather a group of children together in a swimming pool, they're more likely to jump and splash about than swim lengths but it still means they're exercising whilst having fun. Plus, because of the resistance of the water, moving about in a pool is a particularly beneficial form of exercise.

Children's pool parties aren't just limited to playing in the water though. There are some very sophisticated venues when it comes to pools, with attractions such as slides, wave machines and fountains. Some venues also include inflatables, rubber rings, various floats and water containers. A popular addition is the giant inflatable, which adventurous children absolutely love. And whilst we're on the subject of adventure, zorbing parties are becoming increasingly popular. You can find more details of zorbing parties in the case study that I have chosen for this chapter.

The case study in this chapter is local authority based and there is an advantage with this because virtually every local authority has at least one swimming pool, with many of them hosting children's parties. This means that you shouldn't have too many problems finding a public pool in your area where you can hold your child's birthday party. You may also find pool parties run by the private sector, for example, health clubs and hotel leisure clubs so it's worth asking around or trying a search on the Internet. Many venues (both public and private) also have dining facilities and the party will usually consist of time spent in the water plus time spent in a party/dining area.

A lot of pools will have a minimum age requirement or they may require that all children are proficient swimmers. This is one point that is worth checking out. I have given further points for consideration at the end of the case study for this chapter.

CASE STUDY

Tameside Sports Trust at: www.tamesidesportstrust.com/party.asp.
You can either book online or through the specific sports centre. Details of telephone numbers for each centre are given on the website.

The Location

Tameside Sports Trust have various venues in Tameside, Manchester that host swimming parties for children. The locations for pool parties are: Hyde Leisure Pool, Ashton Pools, The Copley Centre and Medlock Leisure Centre, and the types of parties vary depending on the venue. You can find details of the different sporting facilities in Tameside, including pools, at: www.tamesidesportstrust.com/facilities.asp. The website also gives a map and directions for each of the venues.

Preparation

The organisers give out free party invitations to parents as soon as they book a party. It is advisable to book a party one or two months in advance of the event as children's birthday parties with Tameside Sports Trust are very popular.

The Party

You can choose from three different types of parties, but these are not available at all locations. Sessions for all of the parties last for one hour and 45 minutes. This consists of one hour in the pool and 45 minutes in the party area.

Details of the three types of parties, together with the location where they are held, are as follows:

   – *The Swim, Slide and Wave Party* (Hyde Leisure Pool)

This party is available exclusively at Hyde Leisure Pool as it revolves around the facilities that are available at that particular location. These include: geysers, bubble beds, wild waves, the white water channel and the red ripster slide. The party takes place during a general swimming session when these facilities are also available to the general public. However, the party area is available only to guests of the party.

   – *The Wet and Wild Party* (Ashton Pools, Medlock Leisure Centre and The Copley Centre)

With this type of party guests have exclusive use of the pool at your chosen location. The parties are led by a qualified swimming teacher and children can take part in a range of fun activities and games in the water as well as spending time in the party area. Adults can join children in the water free of charge.

   – *Zorbing Party* (Ashton Pools, Medlock Leisure Centre and The Copley Centre)

Guests also have exclusive use of the pool with Zorbing Parties. Children use equipment called Water Walkerz. These resemble a large, transparent ball that children are placed inside. This enables the children to stay dry whilst they have fun rolling, running and flipping on the water. You can find out more about Water Walkerz at: http://www.waterwalkerz.com/. For this type of party children also spend 45 minutes in the party area.

Suitable Ages

Parties cater to different age groups depending on the activities involved. Tameside Sports Trust coaches are qualified and trained to work with children of varying ages. When you book a party the staff give you guidance regarding suitable activities for the particular age group. Furthermore, the team at Tameside Sports Trust focus on accommodating customer's requirements whilst also ensuring that activities are age appropriate.

Food

There are two different options for food, which are: the Light Bite Platter, and Delicious Lunch Bags. The Light Bite Platter is only available at Hyde Leisure Pool and The Copley Centre, whereas Delicious Lunch Bags are available at all venues. Details of the two options are as follows:

- *Light Bite Platter* – Food is served on platters, buffet style so children have a selection of foods. The platters include: delicious sandwiches and wraps with different fillings of cheese, tuna, ham and jam; chips; chicken bits; and unlimited cordial.
- *Delicious Lunch Bags* – With the lunch bags the children each choose one type of sandwich from the selection of tuna, ham, cheese and jam. They also receive a packet of crisps, yoghurt stick and Fruit Shoot drink. The party organisers need to notify the venue of the sandwich selections at least 24 hours before the party.

How many Children?

The number of children that can attend depends on the type of party and the size of the activity area at the location where the party is being held. This applies to both minimum numbers and maximum numbers. On average parties usually cater for at least 10 children with a maximum of around 30.

Cost

The costs for the Swim, Slide and Wave Party and the Wet and Wild Party are £8.50 per person. This price is fully inclusive of activities, and food and drink, as described above. An additional one off payment of £50.00 is charged for zorbing parties as this type of party requires extra staff to comply with health and safety requirements.

There are a number of optional extras as follows:

- Bite size treats platter from £1.00 per child, which consists of a selection of mini cakes, and sweets such as Haribo.
- Goody bags at £1.25 per person. Boys receive a 'pirate' bag and girls receive a 'princess' bag. Both types of party bags include colouring books and crayons, a (make your own) hat or tiara, stickers, a game and a jigsaw. Parents have the option of bringing their own party bags or adding to the contents of the 'pirate' or 'princess' party bags.
- Refreshments for parents and other adults. These start at £1.50 per cup of tea or coffee, and platters of sandwiches and wraps, which are charged at £3 per adult.

What's Included?

Apart from the optional extras described in the previous section, each party includes:

- One hour in the water
- 45 minutes in the party room
- A Party Host
- Birthday balloons
- Party invitations
- Food as described above
- A personalised birthday poster on display for the birthday boy or girl
- A free swimming voucher for the birthday child

Adults can join children in the pool for free; this applies to each of the types of parties. Parents can even have a go at zorbing as the Water Walkerz are also suitable for adults. However, as time in the Water Walkerz is limited, in practice parents do not usually participate in zorbing.

Points to Consider

Tameside Sports Trust does not supply birthday cake or candles so you will have to bring your own as well as some serviettes to wrap the cake. Staff at Hyde Leisure Pool and the Copley Centre are happy to cut the cake into portions for each child, wrap it in serviettes and place one portion into each party bag. It's also a good idea to let parents know that their children will need a £1 coin or token for the lockers.

Chapter 3: Discover a Pop Star

Pop Star Parties

OVERVIEW

With so much focus on celebrities nowadays, children will love the chance to be a pop star for a day. Although many parents and grandparents may not agree with celebrity culture, the fact is that it's here and there's no getting away from it. If all your children's friends are interested in pop stars then the chances are that your children will want to take an interest too. This type of party will not generally be suitable for very young children and the case study we have featured offers parties for children from eight years of age.

Pop star parties are a really fun occasion for children and, although they will mainly appeal to girls, there is no reason why boys can't get involved too. The parties usually involve choosing one or more songs, practicing, and then recording the song or songs using studio recording equipment. The children attending the party will normally receive a CD or DVD of the recording and sometimes photographs as well. As with all parties you may want the children to spend some time eating and drinking. Not all companies provide catering so you may have to organise this yourself, as well as the birthday cake.

We have chosen Pop Star Parties for our case study because the parties are widely available and the proprietor has 14 years' experience in the music industry. Pop Star Parties also offers a very comprehensive party package, which includes extra special touches to make the party more fun, such as a chance to pose on the red carpet. Pop Star Parties is based in the Midlands and has 10 studios nationwide. The organisation also uses 'Pop Pods' to transport the recording equipment so that you can have the party at a location of your choice within a specific radius. The entire area covered is shown on the website (http://www.popstarparties. org).

Pop parties are gaining in popularity and there are other businesses that offer them. Two examples are: Studio One Three in Manchester (www.studioonethree.com) and Born in a Barn Recording Studio in the Midlands (www.borninabarnstudio.co.uk). Studio One Three offers parties for up to three children and the children spend some time in the studio experimenting with different sound effects (under supervision) before recording their song or songs. Born in a Barn Recording Studio offers parties for children aged from eight to eighteen. Again the children have rehearsing and recording time as well as stopping for something to eat and drink. You can either order a buffet from the organisers or take your own, and at the end of the party the children have a disco.

Generally, availability for pop parties will be restricted depending on where the particular studios are located. Our case study features an unusual organisation because the use of 'Pop Pods' means that the party can come to you. However, there may be other businesses that offer this facility. To find companies offering pop star parties in your area, try entering 'pop star parties (+ *your area*)' in an Internet search engine and see what results come up. Be careful to check the minimum age specifications though.

CASE STUDY
Pop Star Parties at: http://www.popstarparties.org.
Email: Mark@popstarparties.org.
Tel: Mark Newton on 01386 700640 or 07828 600443.

The Location
Pop Star Parties is based in the Midlands with 10 recording studios nationwide.

The company also has a number of 'Pop Pods' which travel to different areas of the country. Areas that fall within a specific radius (shown as a green circle on the website) are included in the price of the party. However, for areas outside of this radius there is an additional charge to meet extra fuel costs in relation to transporting the Pop Pods. You can check if your area falls within the green circle by checking the locations page of the website.

Preparation

You can book a pop party with Pop Star Parties by going to the booking form page of the website and filling in your details. However, you are advised to check availability for your dates before filling in the form, and to book early. Bookings are usually taken two to three months before the party and you will need to pay a deposit of £50.00, with the remaining balance due on the day of the party.

As well as filling in the usual details on the booking form such as your child's name, the date and time of the party, age of the birthday child and number of children attending, you will also be asked a few other details. These details include whether you want to host your child's party at the Pop Star Parties studios or at your own chosen location.

Pop Star Parties can come to you thanks to their Pop Pods which transport sophisticated recording equipment that can be used in the home or other venue. This enables them to provide children's birthday parties in many parts of the country in addition to parties based at their static studios. If you are choosing to hold the party at your own chosen location you need to provide the venue address as well as your home address on the booking form. The equipment from the party pods can be set up in any home but you may prefer to hire another venue if there are a large number of children attending the party. It only takes minutes to set up the equipment which can soon transform the venue into a recording studio.

At the time of booking your child should also choose a song to record with friends at the party, and the choice of song is unlimited provided the lyrical content is suitable for children. After making the song choice your child and his or her friends will be allocated their own web page to enable them to learn and practice the song ahead of the party. Early booking enables Pop Star Parties to load the practice page onto the website well before the party. Pop Star Parties will also supply customised party invitations for each guest which will show the link to the specific web page. It is best if your child chooses his or her top three songs so that the company can select the best one to record once the lyrical content has been checked.

Video Parties

For all parties you can also choose whether you want to have a video taken of the party. This is an optional extra so there is an additional charge, and with this option each child will receive a DVD of the recording. This differs from the standard package in which the birthday child would receive a CDR of photographs taken on the day. It is important to note that if you select the video option on the booking form, you will not be able to cancel due to the costs that the company incurs.

The Party

The proprietor of Pop Star Parties is Mark Newton who is a Music Technology graduate with 14 years' experience in the music recording industry. He is used to managing a recording studio where bands can record tracks, but after he successfully held his own daughter's birthday party at one of his studios he decided to make this service available for other children's birthday parties.

All of the children's birthday parties are hosted by fully trained staff who will stay for the duration of the party and keep the children entertained. Children's parties last for two hours including time spent eating. However, Pop Star Parties does not take care of the catering so you will have to make your own arrangements. This applies to parties at your own chosen venue as well as parties at the recording studios. If you choose to have your child's birthday party at the studios you will have access to the green room for eating and drinking and the company will dispose of all rubbish afterwards.

The party fun starts with a walk down the red carpet together with a pose for the cameras before being issued with a 'VIP pass' to the party. Children attending the party can then enjoy a glass of non-alcoholic champagne. Recording begins once the children have had a quick practice. The children will sing the song that was chosen before the party so they should have learnt the song beforehand. They will sing as a group and the recording sessions last for half an hour using high tech microphones. After the children have recorded their disc they can take part in some disco karaoke.

Following the recording session there is a mock presentation ceremony for 'best single of the year'. At the end of the party the children will each receive a custom-printed CD of the recording. The birthday child will also receive a framed disc and a CDR containing photographs of the party. However, if you opt for a video party this doesn't include the CDR; instead every child will receive a DVD of the party.

Suitable Ages

The parties are suitable for children from the age of 8 and there is no upper age limit.

Food

Pop Star Parties does not take care of catering so you will have to make your own arrangements for all types of parties.

How many Children?

Parties can be held for as few as 2 children. The maximum number of children that can attend is 30.

Cost

Costs depend on the type of party and are as follows:

Pop Pod Parties

The parties at your chosen location cost £230.00 for up to 10 children. For numbers in excess of 10, a charge of £10.00 for each additional child will apply.

Studio Parties

For studio parties it costs around £330.00 for 10 children, with a charge of £10.00 per head for each additional child.

Video Parties

For video parties an additional charge of £100.00 per party applies.

What's Included?

All of the children attending a birthday party will receive:

- A party invitation with a web link to the practice page to enable them to practice the song before the party takes place
- A glass of non-alcoholic champagne
- A 'VIP pass'
- A custom printed CD of the song recording

The birthday child will receive:

- A framed disc
- A CRD of the photographs taken during the party

Optional Extras

For video parties each of the children will receive a DVD recording of the party but the CRD for the birthday child is not included with this option.

Points to Consider

If you want a birthday cake or party bags for your child's party, you will need to provide these as well as candles, serviettes and a knife to cut the cake.

It is important to note that the number of children you enter on the booking form is the number that you will be charged for on the day of the party. This is because all the CDs are custom printed and ordered in advance.

Chapter 4: Get your Skates on

Ice Skating and Roller Skating Parties

OVERVIEW

The good thing about ice skating and roller skating is that most children will get the hang of it within an hour. However, it may be worthwhile warning the parents if you are thinking of having a skating party as it will give them an opportunity to let their children try it out beforehand if they want. This will help the children to get the most out of the party. Once they have learnt how to skate most children will find it exciting and exhilarating. It is also likely to appeal equally to boys and girls.

The availability of ice skating and roller skating rinks will vary throughout the country so it is best to check availability in your area before deciding on a party of this type. We have based our case study on Silver Blades ice rinks, which have five different centres in various parts of the country, but some other organisations you could try are:

- *Roller Disco* (www.rollerdisco.com) – hosts children's roller skating birthday parties and has centres in Kent, Surrey, Sussex and Hertfordshire.

- *Skater Club* (http://skatersclub.btck.co.uk/) – is based in the Midlands and the North East and provides a choice of children's roller skating birthday parties. They also offer mobile parties, which can be held at your own chosen venue.
- *Alexandra Palace* in North London (http://www.alexandrapalace. com/ice-rink/) – holds children's ice skating birthday parties at the weekends.

One point to bear in mind with skating is that the children will need to be dressed appropriately. With this type of activity the participants sometimes collide or fall over so it may be best to be aware of this, and some centres may require the children to wear protective clothing. Also, for ice skating the children will need to be well wrapped up to keep warm.

CASE STUDY

Silver Blades Ice Rinks at: http://silver-blades.co.uk/. There are a total of 5 branches and this case study is based on the Altrincham venue, but all venues have similar arrangements.

The Location

Silver Blades Ice Rinks are situated in Cannock (Staffordshire), Altrincham (Cheshire), Gillingham (Kent), Leeds (Yorkshire – opening late 2013) and Widnes (Cheshire). From the home page of the Silver Blades website (http://silver-blades.co.uk/) select a region and you will be taken to the website for that particular venue. You will then find details of the address and a map on the contact page.

Preparation

It is advisable to book your child's party at least two months in advance as this will give you a greater choice regarding dates and times. You can book a party as little as two weeks beforehand but this will be subject to availability. Once you have booked the party, your invitations will be sent to you or you can arrange to collect them at the ice rink.

The Party

With Silver Blades birthday parties children skate for one hour prior to eating. They then spend approximately 30 minutes in the party room where they will eat. After they have finished their food they can go on the ice again for as long as they want until the session finishes. So, for example, if you have your child's birthday at the weekend, public skating sessions finish at 4pm. Therefore, even if your child's party was booked for the morning, the children would still be able to stay on the ice until 4pm.

Suitable Ages

There are no age limits for birthday parties, as the parties are suitable for children at all ages.

Food

Children have a choice of hot or cold food. The cold food is buffet style with a selection of sandwiches. With the hot food children can choose between a burger, hotdog or pizza, all of which are served with chips. Children will also have fruit squash to drink.

How many Children?

The minimum number of children that can attend a birthday is 10 and the maximum is 15. If the number of children attending your child's party will be more than 15 it is still possible to arrange a party, but this will be in the bar area as the party room is not large enough to accommodate more than 15 children.

Cost

Birthday parties cost £12.00 per child.

There are also a number of extras available, as follows:

A birthday announcement, which appears on a moving sign - £2.00.

Skating aids (per below) throughout the party - £5.00 each.

Coaching session with a qualified NISA coach – £15.00 for 30 minutes.

Ice skates – from £45.00 a pair.

Birthday cake - £10.00.

Photograph of the party in a Silver Blades frame - £4.00.

What's Included?

The following are included in the cost of a children's party:

- Food and drink as described above
- Separate party room and host
- Invitations
- Admission to the ice rink plus skate hire
- A Silver Blades Goody Bag
- A free hot drink for accompanying adults (one adult per child)

Points to Consider

The venue does not provide the birthday cake so you will have to purchase this separately. However, staff will supply candles, serviettes and a knife if necessary.

Another point to consider is that children will need to wear warm clothing and bring gloves with them to wear on the ice.

Chapter 5: Score some Goals

Football Parties

OVERVIEW

This type of party is bound to appeal to the majority of boys although, as the UK's most popular sport, football will probably attract some girls too. If you are planning to invite girls to your child's party, then it is best to check whether the party is likely to appeal to them before making your booking. Otherwise you may end up with a situation where lots of guests are turning down the invitation because they do not want to play football. This in turn could lead to disappointment for your child.

There is now an abundance of private football clubs in the UK. Many of them offer football coaching for children, and a number of them host children's football birthday parties. We have included Powerleague's birthday parties in our case study because they are widely available, with 45 venues in the UK, but there are others you could try. Some private football coaching clubs operate more widely than others; another two of the major ones you could try are: Goals Soccer Centres (www.goalsfootball.co.uk) and Little Kickers (www.littlekickers.co.uk).

You should note that where some private companies have their own venues, others will use public venues such as school playing fields and sports halls. The organisation featured in our case study caters for seven-a-side and five-a-side football but there are other football party providers that specialise in 11-a-side.

Apart from private clubs, you could try your local authority sports centres. However, they would be more likely to provide birthday parties related to sport in general rather than football alone. Another option is professional football clubs as some of these offer children's birthday parties. For example, Chelsea Football Club (www.chelseafc.com) holds children's birthday parties, which include a tour of the stadium as well as a game of five-a-side football.

A point worth checking is whether the games of football will be held indoors or outdoors, because children are likely to get messier in adverse weather conditions if they are playing outside. The organisation that we have chosen for our case study has indoor soccer domes at some of its centres, but not all of them.

CASE STUDY

Powerleague at: http://www.powerleague.co.uk/.

There are 46 different Powerleague venues throughout the UK. Parties vary depending on the venue, so the case study below represents a generalisation of what is included in a typical birthday party. As well as offering birthday parties, Powerleague runs seven and five-a-side football leagues, tournaments and football coaching for children and adults. A number of the venues also have gyms.

The Location

To find your nearest centre, go to the Powerleague website and select the drop down list headed 'Select Centre' on the top left of the home page. Scroll down the list and click your chosen centre. Contact details and information relating to that specific centre will then appear on the selected page.

Preparation

It is best to book your child's birthday party with Powerleague as early as possible because parties are subject to availability at all centres. The minimum recommended time is three weeks in advance of the party as this gives the centre plenty of time in which to make the arrangements and send the invitations out to you. However, Powerleague will occasionally accept bookings at shorter notice if there is space available. It is easy to check availability using the 'Kids' Parties' page of the Powerleague website and filling in the box on the right hand side. You will need to pay a deposit in order to secure your booking.

Birthday invitations are provided by the venue and will be given to you once you book a birthday party and pay your deposit. You can either, book a party and pay your deposit at the reception area of your nearest Powerleague centre, or you can book by phone or online. With the latter two options your invitations will be sent out in the post to you when you make the booking and pay your deposit. Please check with your local centre to find out how much deposit is required to secure the booking.

The Party

Powerleague birthday parties consist of one and a half hours of football-based activity, and the venue allocates a Dedicated Party Coach to supervise the children and keep them entertained, if required. However, this is an optional extra so if you don't choose this option then you need to ensure that at least one parent remains at the party. The venue will organise all of the catering for the party including food and drinks. Generally, the time spent at the party is broken up into an hour long activity session, 20-25 minutes spent eating and drinking then a further activity session. However, this format can be adapted to suit your personal preferences. The total duration of children's birthday parties is two hours.

Football is the main activity that takes place at Powerleague children's birthday parties. The centre organisers work hard to ensure that the party activities are fun for everyone. Therefore, games of football are interspersed with coaching tips sessions and/or optional directed sessions. Your nearest Powerleague centre can explain what the directed sessions involve. Additionally, all the Powerleague managers are trained in first aid.

The centre organisers always ensure that the birthday child is made to feel special and is the central focus throughout all the activities. As part of this focus the birthday child receives a special medal at the end of the party, which is included with the cost.

Powerleague centres vary in the facilities that they offer. Some have outdoor pitches only, some are indoors, and other centres have a combination of the two. However, every centre has all-weather, floodlit pitches that use the latest artificial pitch technology. This means that there are no muddy kits to worry about, and the children do not have to wear any special clothing to join the parties, apart from footwear that will allow them to run about. You can easily check the facilities for each centre by selecting your chosen centre from the home page of the website.

The parties are suitable for anyone who loves football. Whilst it tends to be boys that have their birthday parties with Powerleague, plenty of girls attend too and enjoy themselves thoroughly.

Suitable Ages

The parties are aimed at two age groups, which are 5-12 and 12-18. The prices that we have given are based on the 5-12 age group. For older children, prices vary slightly so it is best to contact your chosen Powerleague centre for further details.

Food

Birthday party food generally consists of finger foods and/or pizzas but this may vary from centre to centre so it is best to check. Your Powerleague centre will take account of your individual preferences together with any dietary requirements that the children may have. Powerleague venues will also provide water and squash to all of the children throughout the duration of the birthday party.

How many Children?

The prices quoted for birthday parties apply to a minimum number of 10 children. This is a set price so there are no discounts if less than 10 children attend your child's birthday party. If you want more than 10 children to attend the party you can add additional children at an extra cost per child.

Cost

Basic prices for a child's birthday party vary between £110.00 and £130.00 for 10 children depending on the venue and its location. If more than 10 children attend you will be charged an additional cost per child. Your Powerleague centre will be able to give you more details regarding this additional price. These prices apply to the 5-12 age group as explained above.

There are five optional extras that you can add to your child's birthday party. These are available across all Powerleague centres and are as follows:

- A football coach – £20.00 per party.
- Medals for all the children - £20.00 per party of 10 children, plus £2.00 for each additional child.

- Party bags - £20.00 per party of 10 children plus £2.00 for each additional child. The party bags are branded, multi-use sports bags containing various quality items, many of which are Powerleague branded. Your Powerleague centre will be able to give you more details.
- A football themed birthday cake - £8.00 per party.
- A football - £8.00 each.

Powerleague also has a 'Take the Lot' option where you receive all of the above five items at a discounted total cost of £64.60 per standard birthday party of 10 children.

Some of the Powerleague centres offer other optional extras based on their location. For example, Powerleague, Wembley offers a tour of the stadium and Powerleague, Newcastle offers a Newcastle theme. It is best to contact your chosen Powerleague centre to get a full idea of the extras that they can offer.

What's Included?

Parties with Powerleague include all food, drinks and party invitations. They also include activities organised by a Dedicated Party Coach as described above, if you choose this optional extra. For each party the birthday child receives a medal/trophy and a birthday card with a photograph. Party bags, birthday cakes and other extras are also provided by the venue at an additional charge per our 'Cost' section above.

As the children only spend approximately 20 to 25 minutes in the party room, Powerleague does not generally decorate it. However, parents can usually bring banners and balloons to decorate the party room if they wish to do so. It is best to check with the venue before the date of the party to make sure that this will not be a problem.

Points to Consider

Some Powerleague venues provide lockers which can be used for a nominal fee. Powerleague will cater to all of the children's needs on the day of the party and if you have any concerns relating to your child's birthday party you are encouraged to discuss them with your chosen Powerleague centre.

Chapter 6: Meet the Cheeky Monkeys

Zoo Based Parties

OVERVIEW

Most children love a visit to the zoo so this type of birthday party should receive a good reception from your child's friends. It can work out expensive though, depending on what items or facilities the zoo includes with the party. The types of activities and food on offer, and whether they are included with the party price, can vary tremendously from zoo to zoo.

We have featured Chester Zoo for our case study as it is a major attraction that allows you to include many extras with your child's party. However, these are not necessarily included in the basic party cost. Although the party package is different to other zoos it will give you an idea of what to expect from a zoo party. If you want a birthday party for your child at your nearest zoo, then it is best to check what is included and add any extras to the party price, so that you will arrive at a projected total expenditure for the party. Where the zoo entrance, food and any other activities are all charged as extras, the amount can soon add up so it is best to balance your expectations against your budget.

The advantage with a zoo party is that there are zoos located throughout the UK. However, the flip side of this is that they are often based in major cities. Therefore, if your nearest zoo isn't within easy commuting distance, you will have to think about how the children would get to the zoo. Will you expect the other parents to drive their children to the zoo or will you provide a minibus or other form of transport?

When zoo entrance is included as part of the party package, it can represent good value for money as entrance alone can be relatively expensive normally. Dudley Zoo is one example of a zoo that includes free zoo entrance, but there are others. Most zoos will allow you to spend all day at the zoo once the party ends, but some may charge extra for zoo entrance.

With regard to entrance charges, another point to consider is whether there is a charge for adults to attend the party. If the children are allowed all day to explore the zoo then this will usually be unaccompanied by zoo staff so you will need extra adults to help supervise the children. In fact, some zoos stipulate a required ratio of adults to children. If the zoo charges an entrance fee for adults then you will have to decide whether you will meet this cost or whether you will ask the adults in attendance to contribute. Some zoos allow free entry to a limited number of adults e.g. Colchester zoo, which allows free entrance for one adult to every eight children.

There are another couple of things to consider with zoo parties. The first is that parties are often at specific set times so it is best to check at your chosen zoo to make sure that these times are convenient for you. The second consideration is that some zoos include activities involving the animals with the cost of the party, and this can be a big bonus for children. Examples of this are panda viewing at Edinburgh or an animal encounter at Newquay.

To find a range of children's zoo parties on the Internet, try entering 'children's birthday parties + zoo' into an Internet search engine. That way you should only see the results for zoos that actually host children's birthday parties. Alternatively, enter the name of your nearest zoo (+ children's birthday parties) and you should be directed to the specific page of the website that relates to children's parties. This will save you the time of having to search through the various pages of what could be a large website.

CASE STUDY

Chester Zoo at: http://www.chesterzoo.org/.
Email: events@chesterzoo.org.
Tel: 01244 398 722.

The Location

Chester Zoo is located at:
Upton-by-Chester, Chester, CH2 1LH.

The party room (called the Jungle Party Den) is located next to the Realm of the Red Ape and the Arara Picnic Lawn. You can find directions to the party room on the Chester Zoo map which is situated near the Main Entrance. Staff members will also be happy to point you in the right direction.

Preparation

Invitations are not provided as standard by Chester Zoo so you will have to purchase these separately. However, there is an option to purchase an invitation template, which is detailed in our 'What's Included?' section below.

You are advised to book your child's birthday party at least 10 days in advance to ensure that the zoo staff can accommodate any catering or entertainment requests. As with any child's birthday party, the longer you leave it, the less likely you are to find availability for your chosen date and time. You will have to pay a non-refundable deposit when you make your booking, which will be for the full party package price. This will enable you to reserve your timeslot. Details of what is included in this package are given in the following section, and many food items are charged as extra. The balance of payment will then need to be paid no less than five days before the party to avoid cancellation.

If you need to cancel the party for any reason then you need to notify the Special Events staff in writing no later than seven business days before the date of the party. If you cancel without giving seven days' notice then you will lose the full cost of the party, which includes the party package price and any extras such as food.

To book entertainment such as a face painter or Handimal artist, you should make a request to the Events staff at least two weeks prior to the party. This request will then need to be approved. You will also need to supply details of your final guest count, and order your Zoo admission tickets, ride tickets, goodie bags and food at least five days before the date of your child's birthday party.

The birthday party pavilions are situated a short distance from the zoo entrance and zoo staff will not be able to help you transport any food, gifts etc. to and from the party location. Neither does the zoo provide any equipment for carrying. It is therefore worth considering transportation arrangements beforehand and coming equipped, for example, bringing your own trolley. However, if any of your guests have difficulties walking, the zoo has wheel chairs and scooters available for use and these are located at the zoo's main entrance. You will need to pay a small deposit to use these.

It is best to ensure that all your party guests have an admission ticket before going through the zoo entrance except for children under three years of age. These can be collected from the Guest Services building near to the Main Entrance. Should you need any additional tickets on the day of the party, you will need to buy them at the admission kiosks as the Events Department cannot provide them. If you have arranged for a monorail or waterbus ride during the party then you will also need to ensure that your guests have a ticket for these attractions.

You can download a handy check list from the birthday parties area of the Chester Zoo website. This sets out what actions you need to take prior to the event and the appropriate timescales.

The Party

Chester Zoo offers a standard party package for £150.00, which includes the hire of a party pavilion called 'The Jungle Den' for two hours. This package also includes entrance to the zoo for 12 people as well as ice cream, slush ice drinks, 'colour in' table covers with crayons, and a Kids' Explorer Trail for each of the children. Crayons are provided for use during the party but they must be left on the premises when the party finishes. The Kids' Explorer Trail is a set of questions that can be answered by looking around the zoo. Younger children will need help reading the questions and Chester Zoo Events Staff do not organise the Explorer Trail so you would have to supervise the children as they walk through the zoo.

The Jungle Den has seating for up to 20 people and you can book additional tickets to the zoo for £12.50 per person. Birthday parties take place during specific time slots, which are either 10.30 am till 12.30 pm or 1.30 pm till 3.30 pm.

When you arrive at the Chester Zoo Main Entrance you will need to collect your tickets for the party and any ride tickets at the Guest Services building. You will be able to gain entrance to the birthday party pavilion from 15 minutes prior to the start of the party and will have 15 minutes after the party in which to collect your belongings and leave the pavilion. Unfortunately, if you stay beyond this time the zoo will charge £30.00 for every additional 15 minutes that you spend in the party pavilion. Although the party lasts for two hours in the 'Jungle Den' you are welcome to stay at the zoo all day as your admission tickets will be valid for the whole of that date.

On arrival at the party pavilion, the Events Staff will meet you and will be able to answer any questions that you may have. However, they will not remain for the duration of the party so you will have to ensure that you have enough adults in your group to supervise the children. The zoo staff recommend approximately one parent to every three children but this depends on the age group of the party. If you have any problems during the party there is usually a member of staff available in the kiosk next door to the pavilion.

The two hours in the party den are usually spent eating, and opening gifts. You can bring your own music to entertain the children but you will have to agree the volume levels with a member of staff when you arrive at the party. This is so that you do not disturb any of the animals that are situated close by. The zoo also provides a range of entertainment, which can be purchased as extras and these are described in our 'What's Included?' section below. In addition, there are other extras for when you are outside the pavilion, such as the monorail ride. Likewise, Chester Zoo can provide a selection of food for an additional fee as detailed in our 'Food' section.

If you choose to bring your own food it would be wise to bring a cool box because the zoo do not store or refrigerate any of your items. If you want to store food and other items either before or after the party you will have to use the lockers situated at the Main Entrance and transport the items to and from the party.

Chester Zoo provides basic décor for children's birthday parties so, if you want anything more sophisticated, you may want to bring your own. If you decide to do so it will have to be limited to the table tops as the zoo does not allow you to hang anything from the walls or ceiling. Additionally, Chester Zoo does not permit you to bring streamers, helium balloons, confetti or silly string. The staff always tidy up at the end of birthday parties saving you the trouble.

Suitable Ages
Chester Zoo birthday party packages are available for children from 1 to 12 years of age.

Food
If you are organising your own party food you will find a useful list that you can download from the birthday parties area of the Chester Zoo website. This details the items that you will need to bring on the day such as the cake, cake knife, serving utensils and dishes etc. It also contains general items that apply to all birthday parties including carrier bags to take the presents home. As pointed out in our earlier sections, you

will need to transport your food from the car park to the birthday party pavilion.

It is best to note that, if you are self-catering, the zoo do not supply items such as cutlery, crockery or napkins. Therefore, you will need to bring all of these items with you. Also, the food will have to be prepared beforehand as you will not be able to prepare it onsite and there are stipulations regarding the types of crockery that you can bring. The only professional catering that Chester Zoo will allow is that supplied by the zoo itself. Therefore, the zoo will not permit you to use any professional external catering companies and you will not be able to have food delivered during your child's birthday party.

Chester Zoo has a number of catering options, but they make an additional charge for any food ordered. Details of the food options are:

- ***Children's Lunch Box*** (£4.95 per child)
  - Ham or cheese roll
  - Fruit yoghurt
  - Capri Sun drink
  - Fresh fruit pot
- ***Adult's Lunch Box*** (£4.95 each)
  - Sandwich
  - Packet of crisps
  - Mineral water
- ***Buffet*** (£8.95 per person)
  - Selection of handmade sandwiches
  - Cheese sticks
  - Crisps
  - Homemade pizza
  - Cocktail sausages
  - Fresh fruit pots
  - Fruit Jelly

You can also purchase a number of extras with your birthday meals, which are:

- ***Birthday Cake*** (£10.00)

The birthday cake provides 12 servings and you can choose from an elephant cake or a butterfly cake.

- *Candy Floss* (£3.50 per tub)
- *Marsh Mallows* (£3.99 per tub)
- *Flying Saucers* (£3.99 per tub)

How many Children?

There is no minimum number but the standard party package is for 12 children, so if you had less than 12 it would work out more expensive per guest. However, you can pay for extra guests up to a maximum of 20 as each party pavilion is fully equipped with tables and seating for 20 people. If you need more space, the zoo may be able to find another area where you could have the party, so it is best to enquire with the Special Events Department using the above contact details.

Cost

The basic cost of £150.00 is for the hire of the jungle den for 12 people including other items as detailed in the following section. There are also a number of other extras, apart from food, which you can add on to your party. These are all detailed in the following section.

What's Included?
- *Jungle Den Party Package*

The standard package is for 12 children and includes the following:

- Hire of the Jungle Den for two hours
- Full day admission to the zoo for 12 people
- Slush ice drinks for the children
- Whippy ice cream for the party guests
- Tables and chairs to seat up to 20 people
- Colour-in table covers and use of crayons
- Kids' Explorer Trail for each child – a series of questions to encourage children to explore the zoo

Apart from the standard party package, you can book a selection of extras including food, which is detailed in the above section. Other extras are:

- *Monorail Ride* - £1.00 per person.
- *Waterbus Ride* - £1.00 per person.
- *Face Painter* - £125.00 for the two hours duration of the party.
- *Handimal Artist* - £175.00 for the duration of the party. A handimal artist takes the children's hand prints then turns them

into artwork, which the children can take away with them. In addition, the birthday child will receive a memento in the form of a collage containing family hand prints.

- *Animal Letter Artist* - £150.00 for the duration of the party. Each child will receive a piece of letter artwork to take away and the birthday child will receive a special Letter Art gift.

- *Party Invitation Template* - £12.50. This enables you to have specially designed Chester Zoo party invitations to give out to your child's guests.

- *Standard Goodie Bags* - £5.00 per bag. Contents include:
  - Pencils
  - Animal mask
  - Animal figurines
  - Lollipop

- *Deluxe Goodie Bags* - £10.00 per bag. Contents are per the standard goodie bags but also include a cuddly animal.

- *Costumed Character* - £50.00. The character will be either Tommy the Tiger or Motty the Meerkat, and will welcome the guests to the party.

Points to Consider

There are a number of points that you may want to consider, as follows:

Lockers are situated at the main reception area and these can be used to store birthday presents and other items. You will have to pay a £10.00 refundable deposit to use the lockers.

Parking at Chester Zoo is free, but there is a walk of approximately five minutes from the main entrance to the party pavilion.

Chester Zoo does not permit you to bring certain items into the zoo in order to protect the animals. These include, for example, glass bottles, whistles and Frisbees. You can find full details on the Chester Zoo website.

It is important to only buy the number of admission tickets that you will need as any unused tickets will not be refunded. Furthermore, birthday parties will take place regardless of the weather conditions on the day.

Chapter 7: Have Fun down on the Farm

Children's Farm Parties

OVERVIEW

Whether it's down to curiosity or an inherently caring nature, there's something about animals that really appeals to children, especially if the animals happen to be cute and cuddly. A farm visit is a good alternative to a zoo-based party and can often work out cheaper. Not all farms hold children's parties. However, there are a large number of farms throughout the UK that are open to children. Some of these cost as little as a few pounds for children to visit so it is well worth shopping around. Try entering 'children's farms' in an Internet search engine and take a look at the selection that appears for your area. There are also many websites that provide listings of children's farms as well as other attractions. You could try, for example, www.dayoutwiththekids.co.uk, www.netmums. com or www.kidsguide.co.uk.

Children's farms are also known as petting farms or farm parks and often include a range of activities or attractions that are mainly aimed at children. You may find that children can take part in horse rides or tractor rides; at most children's farms they can pet the animals and in some cases they can take part in feeding. Many children's farms also have an adventure playground or soft play area and a café or restaurant. It would be relatively inexpensive to arrange for the children to visit a low cost children's farm, and then give them something to eat afterwards. If the farm café is expensive you could take them somewhere nearby where the food is less expensive, or even have stage two of the party at your home.

When comparing the prices of children's farms in your area, don't forget to find out what is included in the price. There may be additional charges for activities that take place at the farm and these can soon add up. You could also ask whether the café has set meals and what prices they charge for them. If you want the children to eat at the farm café it would be a good idea to check if you can reserve tables for the number of children attending the party. You may also want to serve birthday cake to the children and have them sing Happy Birthday so it is best to make sure that this is alright with the café staff and that they have no objections to the use of candles etc.

The farm that we have selected for our case study may not be the cheapest available but we have chosen this venue because Willows Farm is a fabulous venue with lots of attractions. Take a look at the interactive map on the website (www.willowsfarmvillage.com/) to see the extensive range of activities on offer. Additionally, it offers a party package for a set fee per child. When you pay for a child's birthday party at Willows Farm you get a lot for your money. This includes party bags and a £10.00 voucher for the birthday child, as well as other items and attractions. If you don't live in close proximity to Willows Farm you may find other farms that offer a child's birthday party package.

CASE STUDY

Willows Farm Village at: www.willowsfarmvillage.com/.
Email: info@willowsfarmvillage.com.
Tel: 0870 129 9718.

The Location

Willows Farm Village, Coursers Road, London Colney, St Albans, Hertfordshire AL4 0PF.

Preparation

You are advised to make a provisional booking as soon as you know the date and time that you want the party to take place. Willows Farm parties are very popular and therefore get booked well in advance. You will also need to confirm the arrangements at least 10 days before the date of the party. Again, if you can do this sooner it will be better.

Invitations are provided by the venue and you will receive these along with the confirmation letter and birthday pack once the venue receives your booking form and a deposit of £50.00. The invitations have an area where each child should indicate their food choices when replying to the invitation. This will enable you to complete the meal choice form, which you will receive with your confirmation letter from the venue. You should bring the meal choice form with you to Willows Farm Village on the day of the party. There is also a space on the booking form for you to give details of special dietary requirements that any of the children might have.

The Party

Birthday parties last two and a half hours in total, which consists of one hour and 45 minutes in the Farm Village and Woolly Jumpers followed by 45 minutes in the party room where the children will eat. Children who are members of a party will wear a specific colour of bib to show that they are attending that particular party.

The party will be allocated one or two hosts depending on how many children attend. There is lots to do at the farm so the hosts will ask the birthday child and parents which activities they would prefer and they will then accompany the party group. After an hour and 45 minutes the hosts will accompany you to the party room.

The activities that the party child (or parents) can choose from include Woolly Jumpers and Captain Chicken's Egg Dodge. Woolly Jumpers is an indoor Play Barn, which has soft play activities arranged in sections to suit different age groups. It has various slides, climbing apparatus and ball pools as well as its own coffee shop. Captain Chicken's Egg Dodge is an indoor play area where children can shoot soft balls across the room. It is themed as a chicken run with yellow balls resembling eggs.

As a bonus, the party guests can spend the rest of the day visiting the farm once the party is finished, as party bookings include farm entrance.

Suitable Ages

All parties at Willows Farm Village are suitable for children aged from one to 10.

Food

You can choose either hot or cold food for the children but you cannot mix the two. With hot food the children have to choose from the options given. The cold food is served buffet style so children can have a bit of everything listed below. The full selection for hot and cold menus is:

- *Hot Menu*

    Chicken nuggets

    Veggie burger

    Fish fingers

    Burger

    Sausage in a bun

    Pizza

Each of these options are served with chips and vegetable sticks.

- *Cold Menu*

    A selection of sandwiches cut into triangles

    Chicken satay sticks

    Cocktail sausages

    Vegetable sticks and crisps

    Cheese portions

    Savoury eggs

All of the above meal selections include fruit squash and dessert.

- *Adult's Refreshments*

Willows Farm can also provide food and drink for adults attending the party, which is charged as extra and is added to your final party bill. Options include:

    A selection of cakes and biscuits served with tea or coffee at a cost of £3.95 pp.

    A selection of sandwiches, hand baked crisps and traditional farmhouse sausage roll served with tea or coffee at £5.95 pp.

    A bowl of french fries containing six portions at £5.95.

    A bowl of potato wedges containing six portions at £5.95.

    Houmos with pitta bread and crudités containing four portions at £8.50.

How many Children?

Parties cater for a minimum of 10 children, so if less than 10 turn up on the day you will still be charged for 10. However, for numbers of 10 and above you are charged for each child.

The maximum room capacity is 40 children and adults, but there is an option to use 2 party rooms if you have a particularly large party, as long as the rooms are available. This would take the maximum capacity of children and adults to 65. N.B. You should ensure that there is 1 adult for every 5 children that attend the party.

Cost
The parties are charged as follows:

Weekend and holiday Premium parties	£17.95 per child
Mid-week parties	£12.95 per child
Toddler parties (up to age 3, term-time, weekdays only)	£9.95 per child
Additional adults/senior citizens N.B. one adult is admitted free for every child	£5.00 each
For disabled children please contact Willows for prices	
For Kosher parties (own catering) please contact Willows for prices	

What's Included?
Party invites, a party bag full of goodies and a helium filled balloon for each child are included in the price of the party. Children have a choice of hot or cold food as described in the above section but adult refreshments are charged as extra at the rates given above. Food is eaten in a themed party room and the venue provides a party host to organise the party.

The cost includes admission to the farm village and entrance to Woolly Jumpers for each child taking part. The birthday child also receives a birthday card with a £10.00 voucher inside. The child can use the voucher for admission to the farm, and purchases from the gift shop or restaurant. For each child that attends the party, one adult can attend free of charge.

Points to Consider
There are a number of points that parents should take note of:

1) It is your responsibility to arrange supervision of the children and there should be at least one adult for every five children at the party.
2) Children and adults attending parties do not have exclusive use of Woolly Jumpers.
3) Height restrictions apply for Woolly Jumpers and socks should

be worn for both Woolly Jumpers and Captain Chicken's Egg Dodge. Children using the slides in Woolly Jumpers should have their arms and legs covered.

4) During the winter season party food is served in the themed party marquee.

5) Willows Farm does not supply the party cake so you would have to bring this yourself. However, the staff can supply candles for the cake, a knife to cut it and serviettes to wrap the individual cake portions.

6) If you want to add any extra decorations to the party room you are welcome to do so.

Did you know?

If you become a member of Willows Farm Village you can get a 10% discount off all birthday parties as well as lots of other benefits. You can find out more on the website at:

www.willowsfarmvillage.com

Chapter 8: Throw an Arty Party

Arts and Crafts Parties

OVERVIEW

Arts and crafts parties are a great way for children to have fun whilst being creative. With the case study that we have featured, the Creation Station (www.thecreationstation.co.uk), children even get to personalise and decorate their own party bags as well as gifts to go inside them. This means that they will have a lasting memento of the party. The Creation Station will come to you, which doesn't necessarily mean that you have to hold the party at home. You could hire a church hall, community centre or other building in which to house your arts and crafts birthday party.

If you prefer to use an organiser that has its own premises, you may find one locally through the Internet. The advantage with the Creation Station, however, is that it has a wide network of branches throughout the UK as well as having a wealth of experience in organising children's arts and crafts parties.

Creative parties cater to children of varying ages and abilities, as less able children can receive more help and support from adults attending the party. This means that they will still leave the party feeling a sense of achievement through their creation (even if they did get a little bit of help with it).

When it comes to arts and crafts there are a wide range to choose from for your child's birthday party including messy play, jewellery and bead making, and pottery. A novel idea is a Make Scents party where children can make bath bombs, lotions, potions etc. The party package can be booked either with or without catering included and parties take place at the Make Scents workshops and party rooms in Hartlepool and Stockton on Tees. You can find out more on the Make Scents website at: www. makescents.biz.

To get more ideas for children's arts and crafts parties you could try www.whatson4kidsparties.co.uk as the website has a section with party ideas and party themes. The website will also enable you to search for party organisers and party venues in your area using specific keywords such as 'arts' or 'crafts'.

It's best to let the professionals take care of your arts and crafts party because they know which ideas will stimulate and appeal to children. They will also be used to the mechanics of organising a roomful of children and coaxing them into structured activities. This can be quite a challenge if you are not used to it. However, if your budget is limited you could always have a go yourself. In fact, the Creation Station, featured in our case study, also provides materials to enable you to host your own arts and crafts party. You can find specific activities and related materials through its online store at: www.thecreationstationstore.co.uk. If you're going it alone, you will need to think about where to hold the party and how to minimise mess. You'll also need to consider how many adults you will need to supervise the children.

It may be a good idea to rope in other parents to help supervise the children and assist them. This applies even if you are having a party organiser. Perhaps the invitation could include parents so that each child gets one to one help when working on their artistic creations. For ideas and inspiration you can find books on children's arts and crafts or perhaps ask your children's school or nursery teacher for suggestions.

CASE STUDY
The Creation Station at: www.thecreationstation.co.uk.
Email: enquiries@thecreationstation.co.uk.
Tel: 0844 854 9100.

The Location

The registered address for the Creation Station is: Inspiration House, Creativity Drive, Unit 3, Woodbury Business Park, Woodbury, Devon, EX5 1LD.

The above contact details relate to the registered office. However, in order to book a child's birthday party you would have to contact your nearest branch. Details of all the branches can be found on the website. The Creation Station come out to you which means that you can hold your child's party anywhere you want such as a church hall, community centre or social club.

Preparation

It is best to enquire about available party dates as early as possible to avoid disappointment. Invitations are provided by the Creation Station who will send them out to you as soon as they receive your deposit towards payment of the party.

The Creation Station staff help you to plan the party so that it is tailored to your child's wishes and requirements. They usually phone the parents or carers a couple of days before the party to finalise arrangements and make sure that you are happy with everything. On the day of the event they will arrive 45 minutes before the party is due to start so that they can set everything up before the children get there. This includes arranging the room layout and the entertainment.

The Creation Station does not take care of catering so you will need to make these arrangements. You may want to choose a party venue that will also supply catering or somewhere that allows you to prepare and bring your own food.

The Party

The Creation Station has been operating for a number of years and has a network of branches covering most of the UK. Its staff have inspired over 105,000 children and families since it began. They also ran the Kidszone for the Olympics so they really know how to provide inspiring fun that girls and boys of all ages will really love.

The Creation Station staff are very focused on removing as much of the stress from parents as possible. They therefore point out that adults enjoy their parties as much as children do. You will have your own Creation Station Entertainer who will organise the party and bring all the materials you need for the activities. Creation Station parties are a great idea for children because they enable them to get creative and let their imaginations run free.

There are three different levels of party to suit your budget. These are called 'Cool', 'Brilliant' and 'Awesome'. All the parties are tailored to your child as well as taking into account the number of children attending the party. Additionally, with all three party options the children decorate their own party bags and make at least two pieces of artwork to take home inside the bags as a special memento of their day. Artwork can involve modelling, creating, crafting, sculpting and painting. The parties also include music, dancing and games, which are all organised by the Creation Station Entertainer.

An original feature of Creation Station parties is the 'Magical Ideas Box', which the children love as they get to discover what's inside. This also engages the children because the party activities revolve around the 'Magical Ideas Box'. For example, it might be a wooden box that the children can decorate for the first activity using paint, glitter and gemstones. They will then take part in two further activities by returning to the box to discover what other magic it holds. So, for instance, it might contain balls of clay that can be transformed into animals. The third activity usually takes place after the children have eaten, and parties last for between an hour and an hour and a half.

The type of box and the activities surrounding it vary from party to party, depending on which level you have chosen and your child's wishes. For the three party levels there is a difference in the arts and crafts materials that are provided. To give you an idea of what types of activities to expect, we have included an example below for each of the three party levels. However, these are just a sample and there are many other themes to choose from:

- *Cool Arty Parties* – For a Cool party with a 'Creative creatures, beautiful butterflies and beastie bugs' theme, a papier mache box would be provided. For one of the activities the children would transform the box into a home for a creature and decorate it. A second activity would involve creating the creature using clay and paint. After eating, the children would take part in a third activity in which they could make jewellery or laser bracelets.

- *Brilliant Arty Parties* – A typical theme for a Brilliant party is 'Create sparkly treasure chests and magical wands'. For this party the box would be made from wood and the children would be able to transform it into either a pirate's treasure chest or a princess's jewellery box. A second activity would involve modelling a clay bowl to put the 'treasure' or 'jewellery' inside. After they have eaten, the children would then decorate their own magic wand with beads.

- *Awesome Arty Parties* – This is the most expensive of the three levels and it enables parents, or the birthday child, to choose from the whole range of activities offered by the Creation Station. For example, a 'Creative Kids' party might involve each child designing a t-shirt, then making a willow headdress and a bracelet.

Suitable Ages

Parties by the Creation Station cater for children from ages 1 to 11. Within this range there are no age limits for any of the parties as the Creation Station aim to be as inclusive as possible in relation to ages, abilities and gender. So, if there is an age gap between your children, they will all still be able to attend the party, providing they fall within the specified age range.

Food

Creation Station parties do not include food or drink so you would have to make alternative arrangements for catering. You can either provide the catering yourself, use an outside catering company, or find a venue that provides food and drink and has an area where you can hold the party.

How many Children?

There are no minimum or maximum numbers for parties and the Creation Station has hosted parties for as many as 70 children in the past. However, when choosing the size of venue for your child's party, you should bear in mind how many children will be attending.

Cost

There are three different levels of parties to suit the hosts' budget and the price varies accordingly. The starting price per party is £100.00 for a Cool party, which would provide entertainment for up to 10 children. Rather than charging for each individual child, the Creation Station have price bands depending on the approximate number of children that you have invited and the party package. This allows for the fact that the number of children that turn up to the party could differ slightly from the number invited. The price bands are:

- Up to 10 children
- Up to 15 children
- Up to 24 children
- Up to 30 children

N.B. As explained above, the Creation Station can also often accommodate parties for more than 30 children.

What's Included?

Party bags are provided by the Creation Station; the children decorate them and make their own gifts to put inside. The Creation Station also provides a Party Entertainer, invitations, all floor and table covers, overalls for the children and all materials used for the activities.

Points to Consider

If your child wants a birthday cake with candles, you will have to bring these to the party with you as well as a knife to cut the cake and something with which to wrap the individual portions. However, party invitations, party bags and party bag contents are all provided by the Creation Station as explained above. The Creation Station will also provide thank you cards, which can be coloured in by the birthday child to hand out to all his or her friends after the party.

A good thing about Creation Station parties is that the Entertainers are all fully trained to run the parties as well as being CRB checked, insured and trained in first aid. The Creation Station places a strong emphasis on making it a special day for all the children involved. The parties have some unique and thoughtful touches such as the 'Magical Ideas Box' and the fact that the children get to create their own party bag gifts and personalise the party bag. Another advantage is that all the products are safe for children to use and non-toxic. Additionally, the paints are eco-friendly and washable, making them easy to remove from most fabrics.

A point worth mentioning is that for younger children it would be advisable to book the birthday party in the morning as they can get overtired by the afternoon.

Did you know?

The Creation Station regularly holds competitions on its Facebook page where you can win a free children's party. You can find out more at:

https://www.facebook.com/thecreationstationltd

Chapter 9: Cook up a Feast

Cookery Parties

OVERVIEW

Cookery parties give children a chance to get creative whilst also making treats that they can tuck into or, in some cases, take home from the party. The party organisers featured in our case study for this chapter, Kiddy Cook, also teach children about the science behind cookery through their 'Kitchen Science Experiment' parties. Kiddy Cook operates on a franchise basis. This cookery group provides all the equipment and ingredients for your children's party, but you will have to organise the venue.

You will also find various self-contained cookery schools that host children's parties. Some of these may be part of a cookery school that also has classes for adults. Often these will just have the one building but it's worth checking out what is available in your area. Try entering 'cookery school + (*your area*)' in an Internet search engine. You could also try the search term, 'children's cookery schools'. Then you can contact those that take your interest to see whether they hold children's birthday parties.

We chose Kiddy Cook for our case study because, although they don't have their own buildings, their children's parties are available in several regions of the UK. Additionally, they give cookery classes and workshops for children in various schools and in partnership with the National Trust, farms and allotments. This means that if your children have an interest in cookery, there are opportunities to develop their skills further.

Of course, you could always organise your own children's party but this could be stressful. You would have to plan it beforehand to make sure that you had all the necessary equipment. Furthermore, you would have to make sure that you could keep the children busy, safe and organised. Cleaning up all the mess afterwards would also be down to you. In view of all these factors you'll probably find it much easier to leave it to the professionals.

CASE STUDY

Kiddy Cook at: www.kiddycook.co.uk.
Email: N.B. To contact Kiddy Cook by email, select 'Find a Class' from the menu at the top of the website, then select your region, and go to the 'Contact Us' page. You will then be able to get in touch by filling in the on-screen contact form.
Tel: 07976 619 648.

The Location

Kiddy Cook is run on a franchise basis and hosts parties at various locations in the UK. The regions that it currently covers are: the North West, the Midlands, the North East, East Anglia, London, the South East and the South West. Parties are not based at one particular venue. Instead Kiddy Cook class leaders visit you at your chosen venue, which could be your home, a church hall, social club, community centre or other building with cookery facilities.

Preparation

Party invitations are provided by the venue and are sent out once you have completed the party booking form and paid a 25% deposit. It is advisable to book your children's party at least a month beforehand.

The Party

Kiddy Cook offers a range of parties and can tailor the parties to suit your requirements. Apart from cooking and eating, Kiddy Cook focuses on teaching children the science behind cooking. For example, they can discover how carbon dioxide makes cakes and biscuits rise, or they can find out the difference between taste and flavour. All the franchisees that operate Kiddy Cook parties are CRB checked and have a basic food hygiene certificate. They are also fully insured.

Kiddy Cook will provide either one or two class leaders to organise your child's party, depending on your child's age and the party option you have chosen. However, parents will still need to supervise the children. For older children attending a cook your own lunch or tea party, the host parents are asked to keep an eye on the savoury food whilst it is cooking in the oven. This is so that the Kiddy Cook class leaders can concentrate on helping the children to make something sweet that they can take home in their party bags. With younger, pre-school children it is important that parents and other adults help the children with some of the food preparation.

Parties can last between 45 minutes and two hours depending on the type of party. The parties where cooking takes place are two hours long. Children will usually cook lunch, tea, or cakes and biscuits, and the party includes approximately 30 minutes for the children to eat either food that they have cooked or food that you provide. Once the party is finished the Kiddy Cook class leaders will do all the clearing up so you don't have any mess to worry about. I have given some examples of party types below together with details of what is involved:

– ***Make your own Lunch/Tea*** – This party is suitable for children from the age of five. The party lasts for two hours, which includes about 30 minutes that the children spend eating the food they have cooked. During the party the children will also take part in gastronomic experiments based around food and cooking. Kiddy Cook supplies the ingredients and utensils, and they help the children to make their own lunch or tea followed by something sweet that they can take home in their party bags. There are a range of recipes to choose from, and favourites include pizza and chocolate fudge cake.

- *Biscuit Baking and Decorating* – This party has been created with younger children in mind and is suitable for children from the age of three. It is a good alternative to a full cooking party especially when there are large numbers of guests involved. The children make, roll and cut out biscuits, which they will decorate once they are cooked, using fabulous sprinkles and sugars. Biscuit baking and decorating parties last for two hours, which includes 30 minutes cooking and cooling time. During this time children will eat and drink. For this type of party you are asked to provide the party food but Kiddy Cook provides the ingredients for the biscuits.

- *Kiddy Cook Session* – For child foodies this party is a great idea. It is suitable for small groups of up to six children from five years of age. You can choose from a list of different cookery sessions, from American or Italian cooking to eggs, cheese or English puddings. The sessions last for two hours and can take place in your home. This type of party usually involves cooking two or three recipes, which the children can then take home to eat.

- *Edible Jewellery* – Children from the age of four can attend this type of party, which is great for boys or girls who want to invite lots of friends. During the party the children can get really creative as they make jewellery using a variety of different foods. The activities last for 45 minutes, which doesn't include time spent eating and drinking. Kiddy Cook provide all the utensils and ingredients to make the jewellery but you will have to provide the party food and drink.

- *Kitchen Science Experiment* – This party is suitable for children from the age of four and will particularly suit those who like things that go bang! The children take part in a range of experiments using items that are usually found in your kitchen cupboards. The activities last for 45 minutes, which doesn't include time spent eating and drinking. Kiddy Cook do not provide the party food or drink so you will have to make your own arrangements for feeding the children.

- *Teddy Bear Picnic* – A recent addition to the range of parties offered is the Teddy Bear Picnic for children from three years of age who need a little help from parents. With this party, children experience the magic of bringing their own personalised bear to life with no sewing involved. They then help to prepare their own picnic food. This includes mini sandwiches using cookie cutters to form different sandwich shapes, and decorating cupcakes using sprinkles and glitters. The children will then eat the food they have prepared during the party, which lasts for two hours in total.

Suitable Ages

For each of the examples above we have given the minimum age requirements. If you want to arrange a tailored party this will take account of your child's age group as part of your requirements. Parties for toddlers are usually aimed at children from the ages of 2 to 4. For primary school children the parties are aimed at the 4 to 11 age band. Kiddy Cook can also cater for older children and offer cookery workshops for those aged 11 to 18.

Food

For the main part you will have to make your own arrangements for catering. However, some parties include food that can be eaten at the party, for example, the 'Make your own Lunch/Tea' party per the above example. It is best to liaise with Kiddy Cook regarding your particular choice of party to find out what food is included.

How many Children?

There are no minimum requirements for the number of children that can attend parties because Kiddy Cook charge per party rather than per child. In the examples that we have given above the maximum numbers of children that can attend are as follows:

Biscuit Baking and Decorating – a maximum of 15 children.

Make your own Lunch/Tea – a maximum of 12 children.

Kiddy Cook Session – a maximum of 6 children.

For all other types of party the maximum number of children is 15.

Cost

Kiddy Cook charge according to the type of party as opposed to charging a fee for each child that attends. The price for each party depends on the location and type of party, but as a guide the minimum price is £75.00. This is for an edible jewellery party with a minimum of 10 children.

Party bags are charged at £3.50 per bag (plus a delivery charge of £5.95). They contain a white chocolate chip cookie mix for the children to bake at home. All that is required is an egg and 40g of butter to enable the children (with a little help from an adult) to make between approximately 10 and 12 delicious cookies.

What's Included?

Kiddy Cook parties include the following:

- Invitations
- Ingredients and utensils
- Aprons for use during the party
- Party bags for each child (at additional cost)
- A wipe clean recipe card for each child
- A Kiddy Cook certificate for each child

Points to Consider

You will have to provide the birthday cake, candles and serviettes in which to wrap the individual cake portions. Another point to consider is that you will need a venue with a double oven.

Chapter 10: Pamper Them

Beauty and Pamper Parties

OVERVIEW

Most little girls love the chance to be pampered and feel all grown up, and this is probably one of the reasons why this type of birthday party is becoming increasingly popular. Although many pamper party companies would probably not object to little boys attending pamper parties too, it is highly unlikely that they would want to. This is therefore worth considering if your daughter has friends of both sexes.

A negative point that many critics raise about these type of parties is that they encourage little girls to grow up too soon and that the use of make-up and other products on little girls is inappropriate. My personal view is that you will never stop children trying to mimic adults. I can remember when I was only eight or nine; a friend and I would walk precariously down the street wearing our mother's high heels and beads. I can also recall trying on make-up at another friend's house. In those days it was difficult to get hold of make-up for little girls so we would resemble clowns with bright red lipstick smeared across our faces and eye shadow plastered up to our eyebrows.

One of the reasons why I have chosen My Pamper Parties as my case study for the pamper parties chapter is because they offer six different types of party aimed at various age groups. Each of the parties are age appropriate and the company uses child-friendly, skin sensitive products. If you have concerns about any of these matters then it would be worth checking with your chosen party provider regarding the products they use and the type of activities that are on offer. Another reason for choosing our particular case study is because My Pamper Parties are widely available throughout the UK because of the network of franchises.

When deciding which organisation to choose for your pamper party, bear in mind that availability will probably be through either a national network or a local beauty parlour. Companies that offer pamper parties nationally generally operate on a franchise basis so you could try entering 'pamper party franchise' in an Internet search engine to see what results come up. Bear in mind, though, that companies operating in this way are likely to host the party in your home or other venue of your choice, rather than having the party on their premises. You will therefore have to think about how you will protect your furniture from any damage. The company featured in our case study provides special covers to protect furniture.

If you prefer to have a party away from your home, you could try a local beauty parlour as many of them host pamper parties for girls. However, many smaller companies are more likely to advertise in the local press rather than have their own website. Others don't advertise much at all and you may therefore find out about the parties by word of mouth or by phoning several local beauty parlours to enquire. One avenue that you could try is www.whatson4kidsparties.co.uk as many businesses are listed on this directory even if they don't have their own website. An advantage with this directory is that you can either enquire by venue, if you want the party on the organiser's premises, or you can enquire by party organisers/planners if you are happy for them to come to your home.

Whether you are having your daughter's party at either, a beauty parlour, your home, or another venue chosen by you, such as a church hall, it is unlikely that catering will be provided. You will therefore have to make arrangements to supply party food for the children, if required, and make sure they have somewhere to sit while they eat, drink and sing 'Happy Birthday'.

CASE STUDY

My Pamper Parties at: http://www.mypamperparties.co.uk/.
Email: pamperparties1@live.co.uk.
Tel: 07583433597.

The Location

The head office of My Pamper Parties is in Birmingham but they have franchises throughout the UK.

Preparation

Parties have to be booked via the website, which also allows you to purchase any extras that you may require. Invitations are free for all parties and can be downloaded from the website. It is advisable to book birthday parties as soon as possible as they get booked up very quickly, especially at weekends.

You can book a birthday party with My Pamper Parties either by phone or by email. Once you have made a booking you will need to confirm it within 24 hours by paying a deposit of 20% of the total cost of the party. This will ensure that your time slot at your chosen location is reserved. On the day of the party you will need to pay the balance. My Pamper Parties accepts cash only so you will not be able to pay the balance by cheque. However, you can pay the cost of a party in full by PayPal via the website.

The Party

My Pamper Parties are available throughout the UK and the organisers offer a range of pamper parties and spa-themed parties. The proprietor of the business is a former Party Team Manager at a well-known nationwide party company and has many years of experience in organising pamper parties. Although the business is based in Birmingham, parties are available throughout the UK through My Pamper Parties franchises.

The parties are for girls between the ages of six and 18 with each type of party being aimed at a specific age group, as detailed in our 'Suitable Ages' section below. Party packages provide treatments that are specially designed to suit the particular age group. Children love to mimic the behaviour of adults but My Pamper Parties ensures that all treatments are age-appropriate and all of the products used for children are skin-sensitive.

The packages offered have been extensively researched to appeal to girls and give them a memorable pamper party. All My Pamper Parties staff are highly trained and CRB checked. On the day of the party you will not have to supervise as the party hosts will take control and will run the whole party. My Pamper Parties supplies two members of staff for each party of eight girls. If there are more than eight girls attending the party, My Pamper Parties will provide additional staff to ensure adequate supervision of the children and the party.

Birthday parties normally take place in your home or other place of your choice and last for between two and two and a half hours. The party hosts use special covers to protect your furniture so you don't have to worry about your home getting ruined. The hosts will supply all of the equipment needed for the party and will decorate the room that is being used. You will need to provide sufficient chairs for the children and have a couple of tables available for use. My Pamper Parties do not include catering so you will have to make your own arrangements for this. There are a number of types of parties available to suit different age groups. Details are as follows:

- *Girls' Spa Party* – The girls are given a bath robe and towel each and the party starts with a head and face massage followed by a hand and arm massage. The girls are then given foot scrub and a foot spa each to use. Whilst in the foot spas they will have a face mask applied and cucumbers placed over their eyes, which makes them feel all grown up. Later they will have glittery nail polish applied to their fingers and toes.

- *Girls' Makeover Party* – This party starts with a choice of hairstyling for the girls, with glitter spray, followed by the application of either glitter or nail varnish to their finger and toe nails. The girls will then have age-appropriate make-up applied and an optional removable tattoo. At the end of the party there will be a catwalk and photo shoot for the girls to show off their new makeover.

- *Princess Party* – These are aimed at younger girls who will receive some princess wings and other accessories before taking part in a fun catwalk. They will then create their own princess crown, which they will decorate with glitter and gems. The session includes party games followed by a makeover for each of the girls, where child-friendly make-up is applied. After a photo shoot the girls will each receive a piñata full of party gifts.

- *Luxury Chocolate Party* – This party combines a love of chocolate with a pamper session. The girls will each be given a chocolate coloured robe and will relax with a foot spa whilst being given a chocolate hand and arm massage, and a chocolate pedicure. The girls will also have their nails decorated. During the pamper session there will be a chocolate fountain and the girls will receive chocolate treats and chocolate milk with flutes.

- *Glitter Party* – The focus of this makeover party is glitter, with glittery finger and toe nails, glittery eyes and lips, glittery hairspray and some removable glitter tattoos. All of the make-up used is child-friendly. After the makeover session, the girls will walk the red carpet, and there will be a bubble machine operating in the background.

- *Sweet 16 Party* – This pamper party is specifically for 16 year olds and each of the girls will be given a bathrobe and some non-alcoholic champagne before having a series of treatments. The treatments include a head, neck and shoulder massage followed by a facial with a face mask. Next, there is a manicure, pedicure and hair styling. Lastly, the girls will have a makeover and they can choose from a vast range of make-up to help complete their look.

It is possible to combine more than one type of party but you would have to contact My Pamper Parties to discuss the details.

Suitable Ages
All of the parties are for girls from 4 years of age except for the Sweet 16 Party. However, particular parties, such as the Spa Party are usually more popular with older girls.

Food
Food and drink are not included with the cost of any of the parties so you would have to make your own catering arrangements.

How many Children?
The number of children depends on how many girls you can accommodate in the party room bearing in mind that you will need a seat for each child. Although the party prices are based on 8 guests, it is possible to add more guests at an additional cost of £20.00 for each extra child.

Cost
The prices indicated below are for a party of eight girls. Any additional children are charged at a rate of £20.00 extra per child.

- *Girls' Spa Party* – £240.00.
- *Girls' Makeover Party* – £260.00.
- *Princess Party* – £200.00.

- *Luxury Chocolate Party* – £280.00.
- *Glitter Party* – £220.00.
- *Sweet 16 Party* – £250.00.

N.B. There are a range of optional extras available through the website including party bags at £40.00 for eight.

What's Included?

For each of the types of parties, My Pamper Parties supplies all the equipment that is needed, and the staff bring it to the party. Details of what each of the party types include are as follows:

- *Girls' Spa Party*

    Use of a robe, towel and slippers

    Foot spa

    Massages

    Manicure

- *Girls' Makeover Party*

    Make-up with face gems

    Hairstyling

    Cat walk

    A photo shoot

- *Princess Party*

    Child friendly makeover

    A piñata full of goodies

    Princess accessories

    Fun catwalk

    Party games

- *Luxury Chocolate Party*

    Treats from the chocolate fountain

    Footspa

    Arty nails

    Massage

    Facial

- ***Glitter Party***
    A glittery makeover

    Glittery tattoos

    Bubbles made with a bubble machine

    Catwalk
- ***Sweet 16 Party***
    Hair styling

    Makeover

    Manicure

    Pedicure

    Facial

    Massage

There is a range of extras that can be included for all types of parties and these are shown on the 'Extras' page of the website. Party bags are included in the extras and the contents vary depending on the theme of the party.

Points to Consider

Along with the food you would have to provide the birthday cake if you want one together with the candles. Don't forget to have some serviettes handy which you can use to wrap the individual portions of cake.

You will need to ask the parents of all children attending the party to fill in a consent form, which must be returned to the party host on the day of the party before the party can begin. If a child attends the party without having a consent form then the host may have to refuse treatment.

Chapter 11: Enjoy Big Screen Entertainment

Cinema Parties

OVERVIEW

This type of party is likely to appeal to children of both sexes and to a wide age range. The ages that this type of party will suit will be governed by the certificate rating of the film. However, it is best to ensure that children are old enough to sit quietly for the period of the film without causing disruption. Also, if children are very young and aren't used to the cinema, bear in mind that they may be startled by the loud noises within the auditorium.

We have chosen Cineworld (www.cineworld.co.uk) for our case study as they have 80 cinemas throughout the UK, and offer a comprehensive party package including food. Another large cinema group that offers children's birthday parties is Showcase Cinemas at: www.showcasecinemas.co.uk.

Although Cineworld provides snacks and a drink as part of the party package, this may not necessarily be the case with all cinemas. It is therefore best to enquire with the particular cinema whether food is included with the party or whether you will have to buy it separately. It is also a good idea to ask about prices and/or whether the cinema will allow you to bring your own food.

If you don't happen to have a cinema that hosts birthday parties near to your home then you may want to think about organising your own cinema party. Many of the newer cinemas are part of large complexes, which also have various restaurants and other attractions within the vicinity. It may therefore be possible for you to book several cinema tickets then take the children for something to eat afterwards. Alternatively, most older style cinemas are located in town centres, where there is a selection of restaurants and cafes. This should enable you to come to a similar arrangement. With this option you will need to ensure that you have sufficient adults to supervise the children and/or help to transport them to the restaurant.

If you're lucky enough to live in the London area then you may want to have a film party where the children take part and have their own movie produced. These parties are made available through www.movie-parties. co.uk, a sister company of the young film academy. Children have to be at least eight years of age to take part. The parties take place either in your own home or a venue of your choice. Parties last a full day and the company provides a crew and all the equipment required to produce and show the film.

CASE STUDY
Cineworld Cinemas at: www.cineworld.co.uk for the home page, or: http://www.cineworld.co.uk/venuehire/partyvenues for parties.

Tel: 0844 815 7747 for customer services but for party bookings use the online party booking form, which is accessed from the parties page of the website.

The Location
There are more than 80 Cineworld cinemas in the UK so it should be easy to find a Cineworld party venue near you. You can find out where the cinemas are located through the home page of the website by either clicking on the pull down list to the right of the page or selecting 'Our Cinemas' from the menu.

Preparation
You can book Cineworld birthday parties as far in advance as you like. To book a birthday party, decide which party package you would like from those detailed below, then tell the cinema staff how many vouchers you need for your party of choice. Each of the three party packages takes

place during normal film performances. You will receive the cinema vouchers as soon as you pay for them at your chosen cinema.

When you decide on the film you wish to view and the date of the party, go into the cinema with your vouchers and redeem them for tickets. The movie party vouchers have no expiry date, but you should exchange them for cinema tickets no less than three days before the day of the party. The vouchers are only to be used for tickets and not for any other purchases. They come as part of a party pack that also includes invitations, land-yards for the children to wear, 3D glasses for 3D films, and food and drink, as detailed below. Land-yards are a form of neckerchief like those worn by Scouts.

The Party

There are three different children's birthday packages to choose from, but there is also an Ultimate Movie Party, which is available for all ages. Details are as follows:

- *3D Film Package*
- *2D Film Package*
- *Movies for Juniors Film Package* – This package is available at the majority of Cineworld cinemas but not all. The films can be hired in at the remaining sites but this is subject to an additional fee of £120.00. Therefore, if you are interested in a 'Movies for Juniors' party it is best to check that this package is available at your nearest Cineworld cinema.

All of these parties include entrance and a Munchbox. The difference between the three parties lies in the type of film i.e. whether it is a 'Movies for Juniors' film, 2D or 3D. The duration of the birthday party will depend on the length of the film and children will normally eat whilst watching the film. Cineworld staff usually clear up all rubbish but it is polite to encourage children to put their rubbish in the bins provided.

It is possible to hire an area specifically dedicated to your child's birthday party at some venues, but you would have to enquire at your chosen cinema as facilities vary. Some cinemas use the bar or an area outside the auditoriums for children to eat their food after the film. This would enable you to also present a birthday cake and party bags for the children if you wish. However, these are not provided by Cineworld so you would have to provide them yourself as well as presenting the cake and encouraging the children to sing 'Happy Birthday'. The Cineworld staff will clear up after the party.

You are responsible for supervision of the children during a party and can invite as many adults as you would like to help with this. Cineworld issues one free parent ticket per party with an additional free ticket for every 10 children attending. Although Cineworld staff are not responsible for the supervision of children they will be on hand if you need any help or advice.

The following sections detail what is included in terms of food, the prices for each party package, and the qualifying numbers and age groups. Apart from the three children's birthday packages mentioned above, Cineworld also hosts Ultimate Movie Parties for all ages:

– *Ultimate Movie Party* - With an Ultimate Movie Party you can have a whole auditorium to yourselves within the cinema of your choice. You also get to choose the auditorium, start time, film and four trailers to be shown before the film. The start times that you can choose from are: 10.30am, 1.00pm, 3.00pm, 6.00pm and 8.30pm.

Although Ultimate Movie Parties can be booked for any age group, the choice of film is subject to certification as are the trailers. Choice of film is also subject to the availability of the films that are currently on release, although it is possible to book classic films for an additional charge. There is a choice of 2D or 3D films, and for the 3D films each guest receives a pair of 3D glasses. These parties are subject to a minimum number of guests.

Suitable Ages

For the three children's party packages the children have to be under 14 years of age. Ultimate Movie Parties are for any age group including adults. There is no minimum age for children's birthday parties as long as the children fall within the age range stipulated by the film's certificate.

Food

Each child attending any of the three types of children's parties will receive a Munchbox, which contains a 46oz bag of popcorn, a packet of Milky Way Magic Stars, a packet of dried fruit and a Capri-Sun.

Ultimate Movie Party – For these parties the party hosts receive a voucher for each guest, which entitles them to receive a regular sized popcorn and soft drink. The hosts will receive the vouchers before the date of the party. On the day of the party your guests will usually need to exchange their vouchers at the kiosk counter, depending on the requirements of the particular cinema.

How many Children?

The minimum number of children required to attend a party is 5 children. In terms of maximum numbers, it depends on the size of the auditorium and how many film tickets are available for a particular screening.

Cost

The prices for the three different party packages are:

- *3D Film Package* - £10.25 per child.
- *2D Film Package* - £8.25 per child.
- *Movies for Juniors Film Package* - £4.00 per child.

Parents can add a 150ml tub of Ben and Jerry's ice cream to the party meal for an additional charge of £2.00 per child.

- *Ultimate Movie Party* - Prices for the Ultimate Movie Party are £11.00 per person for a 2D film and £13.00 per person for a 3D film based on 90% of the seats in the auditorium being occupied by your party guests. If you expect to occupy less seats than this, the cinema manager can quote a specific price, but there is a minimum requirement for the number of guests. For classic films an additional cost of £120.00 is charged, provided the film is available.

N.B. As advised above, the cinema does not provide party bags or birthday cake, so you would have to factor in this cost if you wanted to provide these for the party. You can also add to the contents of the Munchbox by buying extra items from the cinema.

What's Included?

Each film package is slightly different in terms of what is included. The details are:

- *3D Film Package* – A 3D film ticket, 3D glasses, land-yard (neckerchief) and a Munchbox for each child.
- *2D Film Package* – A 2D film ticket, land-yard (neckerchief) and a Munchbox for each child.
- *Movies for Juniors Film Package* – A film ticket to a junior movie, land-yard (neckerchief) and a Munchbox for each child. N.B. Junior movies are now shown at all sites so it is best to check with the venue.

There are also free tickets for parents with each of these packages. Parents will receive one free adult ticket per party plus an additional free ticket for every 10 children booked into the party.

– *Ultimate Movie Party* – Details of what is included in this type of party are given above in our party and food sections.

If you wish to bring your own cake and party bags you would have to discuss this with your chosen cinema. Most Cineworld venues should allow you to bring these with you, but you should bear in mind that you will also need to discuss arrangements for candles, cutting the cake and wrapping the individual portions.

Points to Consider

The birthday party vouchers have no cash value so they cannot be substituted for any products other than those detailed on them. You should also note that all screenings are subject to availability.

Did you know?

Did you know that you can receive a discount if you book online? Also, with group bookings one person in 10 goes free. You can find further details through the website at:

www.cineworld.co.uk

Chapter 12: Bowl them Over

Ten Pin Bowling Parties

OVERVIEW

Ten pin bowling is an activity that most people can take part in. It is fun for adults as well as children, but very young children may struggle to hit the pins with the ball. This is something you should consider as you do not want a situation where the children end up feeling frustrated and therefore don't enjoy themselves.

Look out for bowling centres that cater for children by offering facilities such as lighter bowling balls and a frame to slide the ball down for those who are unable to throw it all the way down the alley. Some centres also have bumpers that can be fitted at the sides of the bowling alley to stop the ball from disappearing down the gutters before it reaches the end of the alley. You may even find a bowling centre that has shorter alleys specifically for children. Often venues that cater for children will have concessionary prices for children too. Check out what the age requirements are; for the organisation featured in our case study the minimum age is five, but others may differ.

We have chosen Tenpin for our case study at it has venues at over 30 locations in the UK and offers parties which include food and entertainment. Tenpin is part of a complex, which offers other activities such as soft play and Sector 7 laser games at some sites. If you don't have a Tenpin venue near to you there are other bowling centres with various branches including Namco at http://namcofunscape.com/, which covers 11 locations, and Bowlplex at www.bowlplex.co.uk, which has 13 locations.

Even if they don't host parties, many bowling complexes have restaurants serving reasonably priced children's meals. Often these are provided by well-known chains such as McDonald's or Burger King, which have a choice of low cost, set meals for children. It may be worthwhile checking beforehand what restaurant facilities the bowling venue has, or whether there are any suitable restaurants or cafes nearby that will allow you to reserve seating for a party of children.

You can find other ten pin bowling centres in your area by entering 'bowling alley (+ *your town or city*)' in an Internet search engine. It is important to note that some bowling alleys may suit adults rather than children. This could be the case if the bowling alley is part of a large bar and nightclub complex, for example, so this is something to watch out for.

CASE STUDY

Tenpin at: www.tenpin.co.uk.
You can send an email to Tenpin by filling in the online contact form on the 'Contacts' page of the website.
Tel: 0871 221 0000 for the booking line.

N.B. The information contained in this case study was correct at the time of compilation, but party packages and pricing at Tenpin are subject to change.

The Location

The Head Office address is: Tenpin Ltd, Aragon House, University Way, Cranfield Technology Park, Cranfield, Bedford, MK43 0EQ.

Tenpin has over 30 centres throughout the UK. You can find your nearest location by selecting the 'Locations' tab from the Home Page of the website.

Preparation

Tenpin provides a host of information about children's parties on the 'Bowling Parties' page of the website, which you can access from the

'Parties' tab on the Home Page. Through a link on the 'Bowling Parties' page you can check availability and price (as the price varies depending on the venue). N.B. We have provided some details regarding prices in our 'Cost' section below.

After you have checked whether there are available dates for your chosen branch of Tenpin, you can easily book the party using the online booking form. When booking online, full payment is needed. When booking through the booking line or at a Tenpin site, a deposit of £5.00 per child is due straightaway. It is advisable to book parties at least a month in advance. However, some venues are busier than others so you would need to allow longer for the more popular branches of Tenpin.

Once you have made your booking you will receive a party pack containing your invitations and lots of other information regarding your party. Alternatively you can print your party invitations online via the website, or call in at your local branch to pick up a party pack after you have made the online booking. Should you need to cancel the party for any reason, you will not receive a refund for any amounts paid but you will be able to re-book as long as you choose a date which is within six months of the original date of the booking.

Tenpin advises you to check the party confirmation when you receive it to make sure all the information is correct. If there is anything that you need to change you should ring them straightaway on: 0871 221 0000. Once you have received the party invitations you should fill in the details of your child's party so that they are ready to hand out a few weeks before the party. Parents of the children who are invited should also provide their details when they fill in the RSVP.

Seven days before the party you should ring Tenpin on: 0871 221 0000 to confirm the number of children attending, and you should make sure that you have your booking reference handy. You will also have to pay the balance at this point if you booked via the booking line or at a Tenpin site. You should ask the parents of the children attending the party to drop them off 15 minutes before the party is due to start, and to arrive 15 minutes before the end of the party in order to collect their children.

The Party

As well as bowling parties Tenpin offer soft play, Sing Dizzy karaoke and Sector 7 laser parties at some sites. However, for the purposes of this case study we will focus on the ten pin bowling parties since the other types of parties are covered in further chapters within this book.

Tenpin supply one party host for every 12 children and all staff are trained in health and safety. After the children have eaten, Tenpin staff will do the clearing up, but parents are asked to ensure that all the children's personal belongings and gifts are taken away at the end of the party. There are two types of Tenpin bowling parties depending on whether the party takes place at the weekend or during the week. These are as follows:

- *Birthday Bash* – This party takes place on either a Saturday or a Sunday morning at a set time and lasts for about two hours depending on how long the children take to play two games of bowls and eat their meal. You can check the set times at your local Tenpin centre when you use the online booking form. The party includes bowling, music, dancing, games and prizes. A party host provides the entertainment and there is a balloon modelling display. The children will also eat during the party. The organisers often encourage grown-ups to join in the fun and games, so be warned! For this reason it is best to make sure you are wearing comfortable shoes.

- *Mid-week Birthday Parties* – These take place Monday to Friday before 5pm. They are cheaper than the weekend parties and include bowling and a meal. For mid-week parties the various activities such as music, dance, games and balloon modelling cannot be guaranteed and this is why the mid-week parties are cheaper. Tenpin try to include some of these activities if there are enough staff available but they cannot be guaranteed.

Details of prices for both types of party are given in our 'Cost' section below. For all parties the Tenpin staff provide the entertainment but are not responsible for supervising the children. They therefore request that two parents, or other adults, to every six children remain throughout the party.

Suitable Ages
There are no minimum age requirements for bowling parties but they are generally aimed at children in the 5 to 12 age range. The maximum age for Tenpin bowling parties is 16.

Food
The food is delivered to the lanes and some centres have space for tables to be set up for the food. For both parties the meal is accompanied by fries and ketchup and the children have a choice of:

- Beef Burger
- Chicken Dippers
- Fish Fingers

- Cheese Burger
- Veggie Fingers

You can also purchase tubs of ice cream for 60p per child. Each meal also includes unlimited squash, and adults can arrange to have their food delivered to the lanes as well. Food for adults is not included in the cost of the party and has to be purchased separately.

How many Children?

Each party booking requires a minimum of 6 children. There is no maximum number for birthday parties, but you should ensure that there are at least 2 adults for every 6 children so that the children are supervised, as this is the parents' responsibility.

Cost

Prices start at £7.49 for a Mid-week Birthday Party, and prices for the Weekend Birthday Bash are slightly higher. As the cost of children's parties can vary from region to region, it is best to check the website for up-to-date details or ring the booking line on 0871 221 0000.

What's Included?

Weekend Birthday Bashes include bowling, a meal and unlimited squash as detailed above. Balloon modelling, entertainment by the party host (as described above) and a bowling pin gift for the birthday child are also included in the cost of the party. The party organisers at Tenpin will present the birthday cake, although this is not supplied by Tenpin. Mid-week Birthday Parties include two games of bowling, food and drink as detailed above and a bowling pin gift for the birthday child.

Points to Consider

All party packages are subject to availability; it is therefore advisable to book as soon as possible. Parents and party organisers are asked to supervise the children carefully in order to avoid any accidents, as bowling balls can cause injuries if dropped or handled incorrectly. Parents will also need to supply party bags for the guests if required, and the birthday cake and candles. However, Tenpin will provide napkins and a cake knife to cut the cake into portions. In the event of any queries regarding birthday parties, parents can contact Tenpin by ringing: 0871 221 0000.

Chapter 13: Have a Thrilling Time

Adventure Parties

OVERVIEW

There are so many activities that can be termed 'adventure' including Segway, rafting, kayaking, zorbing, go-karting, indoor skiing and lots more. Adventure parties are full of excitement, leaving children exhilarated and eager to tell all their friends about their thrilling, new experiences. Although many of these activities might be more suitable for older children, it is possible to find some that cater for the little ones. The company that we have featured in our case study, Chill Factor^e, is a prime example as it offers a comprehensive party package with a good choice of activities to suit children in various age groups. For instance, children from two years of age can take place in Snow Play parties, whereas activities such as airboarding and snowboarding are suitable for older children from the age of eight upwards. However, Chill Factor^e only has one venue, which is situated in Manchester. If you are not from the Manchester area, you might want to look for other companies closer to home that offer children a taste of adventure.

Unlike many of the organisations that we have featured in other chapters, companies offering adventure parties are generally private individual companies that only have a few venues. Therefore, availability in the UK will vary from region to region. We will include another couple of examples that you may want to consider. However, this is just to give you an idea of the types of pursuits that could be on offer, and they may not necessarily be available in your area. Hopefully, however, this will give you some original ideas, which you can then pursue. For instance, if the idea of a Segway party appeals to you or your child, you can check the Internet to see if there are any Segway parties that take place in your area. You will probably find plenty of venues where you can try Segway, but they won't all offer children's birthday parties. You may therefore decide on the option of booking a separate children's meal at a nearby café or restaurant. Bear in mind though that Segway (and other adventurous activities) can be very expensive, so it's worthwhile doing all your research before agreeing on a particular type of party for your child.

Some of the other companies that offer adventure parties are:

- *Awesome Walls Climbing Centres* (www.awesomewalls.co.uk), which have centres at Stockport, Stoke, Liverpool and Sheffield. The company offers birthday parties with a climbing theme for children from six years of age.

- *High Adventure Outdoor Education Centre* (www.highadventureec.co.uk), which is based in North Yorkshire. The company hosts a choice of different parties for children from six years of age. Activities include high ropes, climbing, abseiling, low ropes, archery, labyrinth, bouldering, sumo and problem solving games.

- *Adventure Parties UK* (www.adventurepartiesuk.co.uk). This company is based in North Wales and offers a range of parties for children of various ages. The birthday parties are either based at the company's 69 acre site, or at alternative venues for those parties that are offered in partnership with other companies. Some of the activities on offer are: paintball, Go Karts, high ropes, and archery.

Adventure parties may take place indoors or outdoors depending on the facilities available at the party venue and the types of activities that are taking place. If the types of activities that your children want to take part in are outdoor based, then you may have to take weather conditions into account.

To find more ideas for adventure parties you could try an experiences website such as www.intotheblue.co.uk. Bear in mind, however, that many of these experiences may not be suitable for children, or may only be suitable for children from a certain age. Also, not all of the companies will feature the activities as part of a birthday party package, but they may take group bookings. This particular website has a section that is specifically for kids and offers a range of children's experiences including adventurous ones.

CASE STUDY

Chill Factor^e at: http://www.chillfactore.com/.
Tel: 0843 596 2233 or book a party by using the booking form on the website.

The Location

Chill Factor^e, Trafford Way, Trafford Quays Leisure Village, Manchester, M41 7JA.

Preparation

Parties can be booked from five days to 12 months in advance although most are booked at one or two months' notice. It is advisable to book well before your party date, but Chill Factor^e can sometimes accommodate requests from as little as one day before the party. It is best to ring the booking line on the above number to check availability as this is likely to change constantly. You can also ring this number to make a booking, or use the online booking form.

All parties must be paid for in full when you make a booking. Invitations are available to purchase when you make your booking at a cost of 60p each and will be sent out in the post to you straightaway. If you need to cancel a booking, change the date or make any other amendments, you must do so at least 14 days prior to the date of the party booking. You should also let Chill Factor^e know about any special food requirements no later than 10 days before the party.

Most parties can be booked for weekends or during the week, with weekends being the most popular time. Pick and Mix parties take place in the evenings at eight o'clock and these are a popular option for older children and teenagers.

For all snow-based parties you and your guests should arrive 45 minutes before the activities are due to take place. The party host will then come to collect you and will ensure that the children are kitted out before the activities start. For climbing parties guests need to arrive 15 minutes before the start of the party. These early arrival times are important because Chill Factor^e is situated in a popular location near a busy motorway network, so traffic can be unpredictable and it can sometimes take a while to find a parking spot.

Boots and helmets are provided by the venue and hire of them is included with the price of the party. All guests should wear warm clothing and gloves. If they forget to bring gloves they can buy some but it will cost £5.00 per pair. Warm jackets and trousers can also be hired.

The Party

Chill Factor^e is located less than four miles from Manchester City Centre. It has the longest indoor, real snow ski slope in the UK, which is 180 metres. The venue offers a range of exciting activities for adventurous birthday parties. Many of the activities are snow based including tubing, luging and sledging, but you can also take part in climbing parties. Full details of each of the activities are given below.

The birthday parties consist of 45 minutes of chosen activities followed by 45 minutes enjoying the party meal. This is with the exception of the ski taster parties and snowboard taster parties where the activities last for 50 minutes, and the climbing parties where the activities last for 60 minutes. None of the birthday party activities require any existing skills. The idea is to allow all party guests to join in and perhaps have a chance to try something new. The hire of all equipment required for the activities, including snow boots, is included in the cost of the party except for clothing and gloves. If you forget to bring warm outdoor clothing and gloves, these are available as extras per our 'Cost' section below.

Each of the parties has a minimum and maximum requirement regarding the number of guests, which are detailed in the section below. During the party you will not have exclusive use of any of the activities unless your party meets the maximum number requirements for that particular activity.

Chill Factor^e allocates a snow host for each birthday party who will greet you on arrival, help to get the children kitted out and supervise them during the activities. After the activities have taken place, the snow host will take you and your party guests to the restaurant where you will all be greeted by the restaurant staff. They will serve the party food and encourage everyone to join in with singing 'Happy Birthday'. All snow hosts are trained in health and safety procedures as well as being CRB checked.

For every party of eight to 10 children under eight years of age you will need two adults to help the children get on and off the activities. The adult helpers also need to wear warm clothing but they will be provided with snow boots. For snow parties you will need two adults per 10 children to help in the Snow Play area. You are not charged for adult helpers but if any additional adults want to go onto the snow there will be a charge of £6.00 each. You will need to book places for extra adults in advance and this is subject to availability. If you want to watch the activities taking place, you will have a great view from the outside balcony but you are advised to wear warm clothing. Alternatively you can watch through one of the panoramic windows in the restaurant or bar areas.

Parties can be booked either with food or without food and different prices apply for each, which are detailed in our 'Cost' section below. You can choose from three menus for the party guests, which vary in price and contents. If adults want to eat during the party you can book a separate table in the Mont Blanc restaurant by telephoning 0161 749 2246 or 2245. As with the parties, it is advisable to book in advance as the restaurant can get very busy. You should book your restaurant table to coincide with the time when the children will be eating.

For weekend birthday parties there will be a snack bar and additional seating for parents within the party room. However, food, drinks and limited seating in the party room are subject to availability and cannot be reserved by any of the adults attending birthday parties. Additional seating for adults is also available during the week (subject to availability), and parents of the birthday child are welcome inside the party room where they can take photographs and supervise the children.

Details of what is involved in each of the party activities is as follows:

- *Snow Play Party* – This party is especially for younger children who will spend time playing in the special Snow Play area. The area has deeper snow for making snow balls or snow angels. It also has a mini sledging track and a carousel.

- *Airboarding Party* – Aimed at older children who can enjoy body-boarding on real snow using a specially designed, inflated body board.

- *Sledging Mix Party* – Children can race their friends as they sledge down the snowy slopes. Sledges include the Snow Zipper, which is a specially made circular sledge that enables you to turn and leave tracks in the snow, and the Snow Carver, a type of sledge that is specially designed enabling you to dodge and weave down the snow slope.

- *Luge Party* – The Luge ice slide is 60 metres long and is the only one of its kind in the UK. Party guests will experience the thrill of a toboggan run using specially designed mats.

- *Tubing Party* – Tubing involves sliding down the special Tubing lanes in a large inflatable rubber ring.

- *Pick & Mix Party* – A pick and mix party enables you to try out five different activities in one session. These include sledging, tubing, the Snow Carver, Snow Zipper and the Luge ice slide.

- *Snow Park Party* – This is a new party which is like the Pick and Mix but runs during the day when the Snow Park is running, rather than having individual activities. You can find more details on the Chill Factor^e website.

- *Ski Taster Party* – This consists of an introductory lesson on the beginner slope, which lasts for 50 minutes. It is aimed at beginners who have no previous experience of skiing.

- *Snowboard Taster Party* – This is also aimed at beginners with no experience of snowboarding and involves a 50 minute introductory lesson. Guests attending snowboarding should have a minimum shoe size of 2.5.

- *Climbing Party* – Chill Factor^e has a 12 metre high climbing wall. Party guests are kitted out and spend an hour with an instructor learning how to scale the climbing wall.

Suitable Ages

SnowPlay Party – From 2 to 10 years of age.

Airboarding Party – From 8 years of age.

Sledging Party – From 4 years of age.

Luge Party – From 6 years of age.

Tube Party – From 4 years of age.

Pick & Mix Party – From 6 years of age.

Snow Park Party – From 4 years of age.

Ski Taster Party – From 6 years of age.

Snowboard Taster Party – From 8 years of age.

Climbing Party – From 5 years of age.

Food
Standard Menu

- *Main Course*

  A slice of cheese and tomato pizza with chips, or pasta in tomato sauce with chips.

- *Dessert*

  Vanilla ice cream.

- ***Drink***

    Orange or blackcurrant cordial.

Supreme Menu

- ***Main Course*** – A choice of:

    Burger and chips;

    Chicken nuggets and chips;

    Hot dog and chips;

    Battered fish and chips; or

    Pasta in tomato sauce and chips.

- ***Dessert*** – A choice of:

    Vanilla ice cream; or

    Sticky toffee pudding.

- ***Drink***

    Orange or blackcurrant cordial.

Superior Menu

- ***Main Course*** – A choice of:

    Cheeseburger and chips with salad;

    Vegetarian lasagne with salad;

    Battered fish and chips with peas; or, any of the following 10" pizzas:

    Margherita – Mozzarella cheese and tomato;

    Americano – Mozzarella cheese, tomato and pepperoni;

    Tropicale – Mozzarella cheese, tomato, ham and pineapple;

    Piccante - Mozzarella cheese, tomato, spicy beef, green peppers and onion;

    Pollo Flamma - Mozzarella cheese, tomato, BBQ chicken and red onion;

    Vesuvio - Mozzarella cheese, tomato, chorizo sausage and red chillies; or

    Vedure e Funghi - Mozzarella cheese, tomato, artichoke, courgette, yellow and red peppers, mushrooms and chargrilled aubergine.

- ***Dessert*** – A choice of:

    Sticky toffee pudding and custard;

    Chocolate brownie with vanilla ice cream; or

    Ice cream sundae.

- *Drink*

  A bottom glass of Pepsi, Pepsi Max, 7UP or Fanta.

How many Children?

The minimum and maximum numbers for each type of party are as follows:

- *Snow Play Party* – Minimum 10, maximum 40.
- *Airboarding Party* – Minimum 8, maximum 16.
- *Sledging Party* – Minimum 10, maximum 20.
- *Luge Party* – Minimum 8, maximum 16.
- *Tube Party* – Minimum 10, and the party is booked in increments of 10.
- *Pick & Mix Party* – Minimum 10, maximum 20.
- *Snow Park Party* – Minimum 10, maximum 20.
- *Ski Taster Party* – Minimum 10, maximum 30.
- *Snowboard Taster Party* – Minimum 10, maximum 30.
- *Climbing Party* – Minimum 6, maximum 18.

Cost

The costs per party depend on whether food is included in the party and, if so, which menu is selected. Details are as follows:

- *SnowPlay Party*

  With no food – £5.00 per child.

  Standard menu - £9.00 per child.

  Supreme menu – £11.00 per child.

  Superior menu - £15.50 per child.

- *Airboarding Party*

  With no food – £15.00 per child.

  Standard menu - £20.00 per child.

  Supreme menu – £22.00 per child.

  Superior menu - £28.50 per child.

- *Sledging Party*

  With no food – £15.00 per child.

  Standard menu - £20.00 per child.

  Supreme menu – £22.00 per child.

  Superior menu - £28.50 per child.

- *Luge Party*

  With no food – £15.00 per child.

  Standard menu - £20.00 per child.

  Supreme menu – £22.00 per child.

  Superior menu - £28.50 per child.

- *Tube Party*

  With no food – £15.00 per child.

  Standard menu - £20.00 per child.

  Supreme menu – £22.00 per child.

  Superior menu – £28.50 per child.

- *Pick & Mix Party*

  With no food – £15.00 per child.

  Standard menu - £20.00 per child.

  Supreme menu – £22.00 per child.

  Superior menu - £28.50 per child.

- *Snow Park Party*

  With no food – £15.00 per child.

  Standard menu - £20.00 per child.

  Supreme menu – £22.00 per child.

  Superior menu - £28.50 per child.

- *Ski Taster Party*

  With no food – £20.00 per child.

  Standard menu - £27.00 per child.

  Supreme menu – £29.00 per child.

  Superior menu - £36.50 per child.

- *Snowboard Taster Party*

  With no food – £20.00 per child.

  Standard menu - £27.00 per child.

  Supreme menu – £29.00 per child.

  Superior menu - £36.50 per child.

- *Climbing Party*

  With no food – £10.00 per child.

  Standard menu - £15.00 per child.

  Supreme menu – £17.00 per child.

  Superior menu - £23.50 per child.

There are a number of optional extras that can be added, as follows:

- **Clothing rental** – You can hire jackets and trousers for £4.00 each or £6.00 for both. Gloves have to be worn and can be bought at Chill Factor^e for £5.00 per pair. If you want to avoid these additional costs you should ensure that you bring gloves and warm clothing.

- **Invitations** – are available to purchase when you make your booking at a cost of 60p each.

- **Birthday cake** – at a cost of £12.50 per cake, which has the name of the birthday child in icing on the top of the cake. Alternatively you can bring your own birthday cake.

- **Party bags** – can be bought for £2.85 each. They consist of a Chill Factor^e drawstring back, which contains a Chill Factor^e thunderstick, a Chill Factor^e charm bracelet (unisex) and a Chill Factor^e key ring.

What's Included?

All birthday parties include the chosen activity or activities for between 45 and 60 minutes depending on the activity, as specified above. Each party is allocated a snow host who helps to kit out the children for the activity.

Parties with food include 45 minutes spent eating and drinking. The snow host will accompany the party to the restaurant and introduce you to the restaurant staff who will serve the meal.

Points to Consider

It is important to wear warm waterproof clothing with thick socks and gloves. Each of your guests will also need a £1.00 coin for the lockers.

Did you know?

The birthday child goes free as standard with all Chill Factor^e birthday parties.

Chapter 14: Take a Softer Approach

Soft Play Centres

OVERVIEW

Soft play centres were introduced into the UK around 15 years ago and they have rapidly become very popular with children and parents alike. As the market for Soft Play Centres has developed, there is now a Play Providers Association, which was formed in 2005. The association has a code of practice for its members and you can find out more by visiting the website at: www.playproviders.org.uk.

Most soft play centres are based indoors, and are therefore a good option for all weather conditions. They are contained in a relatively small area, because the apparatus is built upwards, and children play inside the equipment using a range of slides, tubes, ball pits and other apparatus. As the equipment is soft and spongy, children are less likely to get hurt than they would be with more rigid equipment.

Soft play centres are colourful and therefore visually appealing to children. Birthday parties at these types of venues are relatively inexpensive, and many centres offer party packages that include food.

You will often find an onsite restaurant that overlooks the play area. Many of these restaurants also cater for adults, so it enables you to take a cuppa or a snack whilst keeping an eye on the children.

Birthday parties at soft play centres are aimed at younger children usually up to 12 years of age; alternatively, they may apply a specific height restriction. For babies and toddlers there is usually a separate area with age appropriate equipment so that they don't get injured by larger, more active children. You will find that some centres are part of larger entertainment complexes whereas others are self-contained.

Our particular case study, the Wacky Warehouse, has indoor play areas that are attached to family friendly pubs, many of which also have an outdoor playground. Time on the soft play equipment will usually be limited but with the Wacky Warehouse you have the advantage that children can continue to play outdoors, providing the weather conditions are suitable.

To find a soft play centre near to you, try entering 'soft play centres (+ *your area*)' in an Internet search engine. The majority of soft play centres offer children's birthday parties. You can also use the website www.dayoutwiththekids.co.uk to find centres in your area by selecting the Play Centre icon.

CASE STUDY
The Wacky Warehouse at: http://www.wackywarehouse.co.uk.

General email address: Guest.Service@spiritpubcompany.com. However, to book parties you need to contact your local branch of Wacky Warehouse.

The Location
There are 74 branches of Wacky Warehouse in the UK, which are attached to family pubs. Details of local branches are given on the website by selecting 'locations' from the menu then entering your postcode and clicking 'Search'.

Preparation
It is advisable to book your child's birthday party at Wacky Warehouse at least six weeks in advance, but it is possible to book up to seven days before, subject to availability. Once you find your nearest Wacky Warehouse by doing a search on the website, you will see the phone number of the pub listed. To book your child's birthday at Wacky Warehouse you will need to ring your chosen pub and ask them to put you through to the Wacky Warehouse. When you book a birthday party

with the Wacky Warehouse you will be required to pay a deposit of £20 straightaway (or 20% of the total cost of the party if this figure is greater than £20).The remaining balance is then due on the day of the party. You will also need to complete and return a confirmation form no later than seven days before the date of the party.

It is the responsibility of parents (or other adult carers) to supervise the children who are taking part, although Wacky Warehouse provides a party host to organise the party. Wacky Warehouse requires one adult supervisor to every five children. With toddlers you may find that most parents prefer to stay and watch them at the party.

You should notify the Wacky Warehouse staff if any of the children have special requirements both in terms of diet and special needs in general. Additionally, with regard to face painting, which is one of our optional extras listed below, it is only suitable for children from three years of age. If any of the children do not have permission from their parents to have their faces painted, you should let the party host know.

Party invitations are provided by Wacky Warehouse as are envelopes and thank you cards. The Wacky Warehouse rules of play are printed on the invitation as well as being shown on the website, and guests are asked to familiarise themselves with these rules. You can collect your party invitations from Wacky Warehouse at any time once you have booked your child's birthday party.

The Party

Parties at the Wacky Warehouse last for two hours, which includes time spent in the soft play areas plus time eating and drinking. The staff will do the clearing up once the children have finished in the dining area. Wacky Warehouse soft play areas are particularly well set out and children enjoy dashing about having fun on the equipment. Each venue allocates a party host to help organise the party but parents (or other adult helpers) are responsible for supervision of the children. All of the Wacky Warehouse staff are trained in health and safety and first aid. At the end of the party each of the children will receive a party bag plus a free return voucher for Wacky Warehouse.

During the party the soft play area will be open to members of the public as well. However, if there are at least 10 children attending the party it is possible to book exclusive use of the soft play area. N.B. As Wacky Warehouses are attached to family pubs, these often have an outdoor play area as well, which is separate from the Wacky Warehouse play area.

There are several types of party available at Wacky Warehouse, which are:

- *Wacky Party* – This is the standard party package, which includes a choice of four main dishes and two side dishes from the party buffet, plus a sweet and unlimited Robinson's squash. It also includes time spent in the soft play area.

- *Wacky Breakfast Party* – This party follows the same format as the Wacky Party, but takes place at breakfast time so the food is suitable for breakfast.

- *Wacky 'The Works' Party* – The difference between this and the Wacky Party is that children can choose any items from the buffet selection plus a sweet and unlimited Robinson's squash.

- *Tot's Club Party* – These are specifically for the under-fives so they are available term-time only, Monday to Friday, between 9.30am and 3pm. Whilst Tot's Club Parties are taking place children aged five and over will not be allowed into the Wacky Warehouse.

There are also a number of optional extras that you can add to your party including face painting, helium filled foil balloons, a character appearance, extra time in the play area and a birthday cake. Full details of these are listed under our 'Costs' section below, together with the prices for each.

Suitable Ages

A Wacky Warehouse birthday party is suitable for children under 12 years of age.

Food

- *Wacky Parties and Wacky 'The Works' Parties* - There is a hot and cold buffet selection for both of these parties. The difference between the two types of parties lies in the number of options that are available. Children in a Wacky Party can choose four main dishes and two side dishes from the buffet whereas children in a Wacky 'The Works' Party can choose any items on the buffet. Both parties have ice cream or jelly for dessert plus an unlimited amount of Robinson's squash. The items that children can choose from are as follows:

  Cheese and tomato pizza, chicken nuggets, cheese sandwiches, ham sandwiches, sausage dogs, veggie nuggets, fish fingers, garlic bread slices, munch crunch vegetables, onion rings and chips.

- *Tot's Club Parties* - The selection of food that is available for Tot's Club Parties is the same as that listed above.

- ***Wacky Breakfast Parties*** - The meal consists of sausage sandwiches, mini hash browns and mini chocolate muffins.

You can also pre-order food for any adults attending the party; you will need to ask your party host about available menus.

How many Children?

You need a minimum of 8 children for parties, except for Tot's Club Parties where a minimum of 5 children is required. The minimum number of children required for exclusive use of the Wacky Warehouse is 10. The maximum number of children that are allowed will depend on the facilities at the particular venue. It is therefore best to ask at your local Wacky Warehouse.

Cost

The charges for each party depend on the type of party and are as follows:

- ***Wacky Party*** - £7.50 per child.
- ***Wacky Breakfast Party*** - £7.50 per child.
- ***Wacky 'The Works' Party*** - £8.50 per child.
- ***Tot's Club Part*y** - £7.50 per child.

You can choose from a number of optional extras, which are:

- ***Face Painting*** - £1.50 per child.
- ***Wacky Helium Foil Balloons*** - £1.99 each.
- ***A Character Appearance*** - £15.00 per party.
- ***An Extra Half Hour Play Time*** - £1.00 per child.
- ***Birthday Cake*** - £9.99.

For an additional cost of £1.50 per child you can update your child's birthday party to a Wacky Wacky Party, which will include a helium filled balloon and face painting for every child.

What's Included?

All parties include the following:

- Party food and drink as detailed in the above 'Food' section
- Invitations, envelopes and thank you cards
- A party bag for each child
- A free return admission voucher for each child
- A party host for the duration of the party

You can also pay for a range of optional extras, which we have included in our 'Cost' section above.

Points to Consider

You will need to bring your own candles for the birthday cake, but Wacky Warehouse will provide serviettes to wrap it in, and the pub restaurants have knives available to cut the cake into portions. If you wish to take photographs you should consider the privacy of other people who may be in the vicinity. The food provided for birthday parties is prepared in an environment where it may come into contact with nuts, seeds, gluten or lactose. Therefore, Wacky Warehouse cannot guarantee that the dishes are free of any traces of these allergens. If you have any concerns regarding this matter you should speak to your Wacky Warehouse party host.

> ## Don't forget!
> *Each child attending a party at Wacky Warehouse receives a voucher for free entry the next time they visit Wacky Warehouse.*

Chapter 15: Explore the Outdoors

Parks and Outdoors

OVERVIEW

Parties at parks are held mainly outdoors, which gives children a chance to run around and explore. Outdoor parties cover a broad spectrum; from organised ranger-led activities offered by some parks to parties that you organise yourself. Having a party in the open air is a healthy alternative, which enables children to become active. These parties can be really enjoyable for energetic, adventurous children but it is sensible to plan for the possibility of unpredictable weather conditions on the day. In view of this, it may be a good idea to send invitations with a note advising parents that children may get mucky and therefore need to be dressed appropriately. This should ensure that parents are prepared if their children return home in wet or muddy clothing.

The parks that we have featured in our case study are country parks in Warwickshire, which generally have colourful Education Rooms. These allow for self-catering, enabling you to provide party food for your children and their guests. The children are likely to spend part of their time indoors as well as outdoors. During their time outdoors they will be involved in interesting, ranger-led activities. This means that the children can have lots of fun whilst getting involved with nature.

You may find other large country parks with similar provisions. Another example is Kent country parks, which offer birthday parties with a one hour activity led by a park ranger. You can find out more through the leisure and culture section of Kent County Council's website at: www.kent.gov.uk.

Many local authorities offer ranger-led activities for children, either within country parks, forests or the countryside generally. The advantage with large public parks is that many of them have a café or tea-room so you can arrange for the children to have something to eat. If you are taking a large group of children into a park café though, it is best to check that the café has the capacity to seat them all. Better still, you could enquire whether they will accept a group booking and allow you to present a birthday cake while the children sing Happy Birthday.

Most local council websites have an A-Z of council services, which you can check to see what is listed under parks and recreation, countryside services, or similar search terms. You can find your local authority using the link: www.gov.uk/find-your-local-council. You may even find some public parks that organise indoor activities in inclement weather.

If your local parks don't have ranger-led activities then perhaps you could arrange your own entertainment for the children. You could try allowing some time on the playground, or organising ball games, running races, group games or nature based activities, for example. You can get plenty of ideas for things to do in woodlands, including activities specifically for children, at the website: www.visitwoods.org.uk. Bear in mind, however, that if you are organising your own activities, you will need other adults to help you supervise the children.

After your organised activities you may want to have a picnic on the grass. Providing the weather conditions are suitable this could be a fun and low-cost birthday party option. Make sure that you come prepared though. You will need to think about transporting the food to a suitable picnic area. You may also need one or more cool boxes to keep the food fresh, especially in hot weather.

Another advantage of having a park or outdoor based party is availability. Most areas have either public parks, woodlands or green areas. Therefore, it's well worthwhile exploring what is out there and what facilities they offer. You can then decide whether it is a viable option and, if so, how much of the organising you will have to take on board yourself. An outdoor party is also likely to appeal to a wide age range of children from toddlers to early teens.

CASE STUDY

Warwickshire Country Parks at:
http://countryparks.warwickshire.gov.uk/.
Email: parks@warwickshire.gov.uk.

Tel: 01827 872660 for Kingsbury Water Park.

Tel: 024 7630 5592 for Ryton Pools Country Park.

Tel: 01827 897438 for Pooley Country Park.

The Location

- *Kingsbury Water Park* - Bodymoor Heath, Sutton Coldfield, West Midlands, B76 0DY.

- *Ryton Pools Country Park* - Ryton Road, Bubbenhall, Coventry, CV8 3BH.

- *Pooley Country Park* - Pooley Lane, Polesworth, Warwickshire, B78 1JA.

N.B. There are several other country parks in Warwickshire but these are the three that host children's birthday parties.

Preparation

Parties can be booked by phoning the relevant venue using the telephone numbers above. It is advisable to book birthday parties as soon as possible as they are popular, particularly at weekends, which tend to get booked up very quickly. All venues require a £20 deposit when you book a party, and you will be required to fill in a booking form. It is best to check with the individual venue to find out when the booking form and payment are required, but it is generally between two and four weeks before the party.

For Ryton Pools Country Park you can download invitations from the website and print them off. However, for the other two parks you will have to provide your own invitations.

Activities take place outdoors, so you should advise all parents that their children need to dress appropriately taking account of the weather. In the event of severe weather conditions, it may be necessary for the venue to offer alternative activities indoors.

Although the party activities are led by rangers, they are not responsible for supervision of the children. You should therefore make arrangements for sufficient adults to attend the party so that they can help to look after the children. You can obtain details of the required ratios of adults to children from the venues.

The Party

The three parks in Warwickshire that hold children's birthday parties provide a range of country park-based activities. These activities are risk assessed and the rangers are experienced in working with children. The parties last for two hours with approximately an hour of that time spent on the chosen activity. The remainder of the time is spent in the park Education Rooms where children will enjoy their party food. The party rooms are colourfully decorated with children's creations showing the flora and fauna of the parks. If you wish to add further decorations such as balloons and banners you can do so. However, parents are responsible for clearing the party room at the end of the party, and all venues supply cleaning equipment to enable parents to leave the room clean and tidy.

Each park varies slightly in what it offers because the facilities at the parks differ. There are a wide range of enjoyable activities suitable for different age groups but some activities aren't available at all venues. Here is an idea of some of the activities that are available at all parks; you can obtain full details by downloading a pdf for the relevant park from the parties page of the Warwickshire Country Parks website at the above web address. There is a link to the parties page halfway down the home page of the website.

-   *Minibeasts* – Children help the ranger to hunt for, and discover, bugs, beetles and butterflies.
-   *Wild Woods* – This party involves having lots of fun in the woods; mud painting, building dens, digging for treasure, making homes for woodland animals and following trails.
-   *Pond Dipping* – N.B. This is from age three at Ryton Pools. With this party children discover the weird and wonderful creatures that live in ponds.
-   *Den Building* - N.B. This is from age five at Ryton Pools. The challenge is to build the strongest den as part of a team. The children are also tasked with camouflaging it and making their den waterproof.

Ryton Pools Country Park and Kingsbury Water Park have miniature trains, enabling these venues to offer train-based parties as well.

Suitable Ages

Parties are for children at primary school age. The minimum age requirements depend on the type of party with activities suitable for different age groups. The minimum age at which children can take part in certain activities is 3. Specific details of the activities for each age group are available from the venues.

Food

Birthday party bookings with Warwickshire Country Parks do not include food and drink, and you will have to organise this separately. You can either bring your own food and drink or make arrangements with the park cafés, which are run as individual businesses and therefore have to be contacted directly. Details of the park cafés are as follows:

- ***Kingsbury Water Park*** – You can arrange to have the party food provided by the country park café, by getting in touch with them on: 01827 874 823.
- ***Ryton Pools Country Park*** – Ryton café is shut at the moment and is being rebuilt.
- ***Pooley Country Park*** – This park has a tea room so you could contact the staff to see if they will provide the catering for your child's party. The number to contact is: 01827 897438. However, the tea rooms are only open at weekends, bank holidays and Warwickshire School holidays, but you can leave a message on the answerphone if you call outside these hours.

How many Children?

There are no minimum numbers for parties since the parties are charged at a set fee. Maximum numbers vary according to the venue and the type of party, but as a guide these are as follows:

- ***Kingsbury Water Park*** – Between 15 and 20 children depending on the activities.
- ***Ryton Pools Country Park*** – Between 10 and 20 children depending on the type of party.
- ***Pooley Country Park*** – Between 15 and 20 children depending on the activities.

Cost

The average cost of a party is £80.00. However, this is subject to change so it is best to contact the venue for up-to-date details.

Party bags are also available at an additional cost of £2.00 per child and contain a range of items. You can find out details of the party bag contents by contacting the venues on the above telephone numbers.

What's Included?

Parties last for two hours, which includes at least one hour spent on ranger-led activities, and the remainder of the time in the Education Rooms. None of the party costs include food but separate arrangements can be made – please refer to our 'food' section for more details. Each party is allocated one ranger and any equipment needed for the party activities is also included in the cost of the party. The parties also include free use of a tea urn, fridge, crockery and cutlery.

Parking for the party organiser is free of charge and the parents or carers of the party child are advised to report to the parks' Information Centre or reception area to make arrangements for free car parking.

Ryton Pools Country Park provides toddler toys for use during the party if you ask for them. At this park you can also bring children under the age of three free of charge. They will be able to attend the party but will not be able to take part in any of the activities, which are for older children.

Points to Consider

You will need to provide your own cake, candles and serviettes to wrap the portions of cake. Your ranger can help with items like candles or a knife to cut the cake but it is best to bring these with you to be on the safe side.

Although parking is free for the party organiser, other parents may be charged for parking inside the parks so you might want to make parents aware of this. All of the parks close at 4pm during November, December and January, which means that all the park buildings will also need to be locked up. At Ryton Pools Country Park guests are asked to arrive at the visitor centre 15 minutes before the start of the party and, for Kingsbury and Pooley parks, guests are advised to arrive 30 minutes before the start of the party.

Chapter 16: Climb Aboard

Transport Based Parties

Image Supplied by Avon Valley Railways

OVERVIEW

There is such a wide range of options with transport based parties; trains, boats, planes, buses and barges as well as others. So, for children that have a fascination for train or plane spotting, a transport based party could be an excellent choice. Transport based parties can either involve a trip, use static transport or take place in an environment that involves transportation. Our case study involves a trip, but we'll also look at other alternatives.

For our case study I have featured Avon Valley Railway, which hosts children's birthday parties on specific dates between Easter and October. The party consists of two return train trips, in a 1950s railway carriage, lasting a total of two hours, with an option to dine on-board the train. Other companies offering a similar experience include Rudyard Lake Railway (http://www.rlsr.org/Party.htm) and East Lancs Railway (http://www.eastlancsrailway.org.uk/groups/kids-parties/). For children that prefer boats to trains, check out http://myrivercruising.com/ for details of their day cruises. These include children's party cruises where children get the chance to dress as pirates and hunt for 'treasure'.

If you can't find a company that hosts either children's train parties or boat parties, you could opt instead for a trip with separate dining arrangements using a nearby café or restaurant. You may even be able to get a discount for making a party booking. With parties involving trips it is important to think about the safety aspect so you will need to ensure that children are adequately supervised.

For static children's birthday parties using vehicles, take a look at the big red party bus (http://www.thebigredpartybus.co.uk/). The bus is specially kitted out for children's parties, with a ball pool and slide. Because the party is based on a bus, the party organisers can come to you and they cover many areas around the Midlands. Another alternative is a party involving a fire engine. Check the Hot Hire website for details of their children's parties at http://www.hot-hire.co.uk/html/Kids.html. They cover the areas of London, Essex, Herts and Kent.

The hire of fire engines and other vehicles is widely available so you can check on the Internet to see which companies cover your area. However, they may not necessarily host birthday parties so you may have to provide some of the input for the children. A further option for children's birthday parties is to visit a transport museum. Again, they may not necessarily host birthday parties so you may have to also organise eating, drinking and presenting the birthday cake. Additionally, if the children do not have an interest in transport, then a visit to a transport museum may not keep them entertained, as it is not as interactive as some of my other suggestions.

Lastly, if the children are interested in plane spotting, you could try holding your child's birthday party at a major airport that has a viewing platform and/or other attractions. Two good ones to try are East Midlands Airport and Manchester Airport. East Midlands Airport has an Aero Park, which is both an aviation museum and a viewing area: (http://www. eastmidlandsairport.com/emaweb.nsf/Content/AeroPark). The entrance fee is relatively low and there are catering facilities during the summer months.

Manchester Airport also has a viewing park and you can find out more at: http://www.manchesterairport.co.uk/manweb.nsf/Content/ concordeviewingpark. The Runway Visitor Park at Manchester has many attractions including a viewing platform, play area, picnic area and restaurant as well as aircraft displays. N.B. Most airports probably won't host children's parties but you could combine a visit to the viewing platform or other attractions with a party meal. Most airports have somewhere where you can eat and drink, but you may need to book if you have a large party, and you should also make sure the restaurant caters for the needs of children.

CASE STUDY

Avon Valley Railway at: http://www.avonvalleyrailway.org/.
Tel: 0117 9325538.
Email: info@avonvalleyrailway.org or fill in the online booking form.

The Location
Bitton Station, Bath Road, Bitton, Bristol, BS30 6HD.

Preparation
Birthday parties with Avon Valley Railway are very popular and are restricted to two a day. They are also only available on dates when the train is not being used for other events. Staff at the venue therefore recommend that you contact them at least a couple of months in advance to book your child's birthday party.

You can obtain a downloadable booking form by visiting the 'Brochures' page of the website. Alternatively, you can contact Avon Valley Railway on the above phone number, or by sending an email to the above email address, or by filling in the contact form shown on the 'Contact Us' page of the website. You will need to pay a deposit of £50.00 to confirm your booking. This is also the minimum charge for birthday parties and is non-refundable.

You can either provide your own food or the venue will arrange the catering. If you want food included with your child's party you will need to give details of your food choices no later than seven days before the birthday party. You will also need to give details of any special dietary requirements and pay for the balance of the party (including food) before the party commences. You can find details of the food choices in our 'Food' section below.

The venue does not provide birthday party invitations so you will have to obtain these yourself.

The Party
Birthday Parties take place in a 1950s railway carriage. They can be booked between Easter and October, but only when the steam or diesel engines are in operation. There are two birthday party sessions a day, which are from 11am to 1.15pm and from 2.45pm to 5pm.

During the birthday party the guests will be able to enjoy two return trips; one to Oldland Common Platform and the other to Avon Riverside. The total time spent on the train is just over two hours. If you want to decorate the birthday party carriage with balloons and banners, the railway company are happy for you to do so. However, you are asked not to use sellotape as it damages the varnish on the walls of the carriages; blue tack or string is fine.

Whilst Avon Railway provides the environment for the party, they are not responsible for supervision of the children. You should therefore ensure that there are sufficient adults at the party to help out. The normal ratio is one adult for every four to five children.

Parents can bring their own food onto the train or purchase it from Avon Valley Railway. Children's party menus are shown in our 'Food' section below. The railway company supplies black bags for you and the other adults to clear away most of the rubbish.

The venue does not supply a specific member of staff to look after the party, but there is a Guard and a Ticket Inspector aboard the train. All of the Avon Railway staff are specifically trained in the appropriate aspects of their jobs.

Suitable Ages

There are no specific age requirements for the parties as long as the party guests are children, as Avon Valley Railway does not cater for 18th or 21st birthday parties.

Food

If you opt to let Avon Valley Railway do the catering you will have two menu choices, as follows:

1) A birthday box priced at £2.95 per child – this contains a small filled roll, a piece of fruit, crisps, a chocolate crispy bar and a drink.

2) A hot meal priced at £3.50 per child – with this option children can choose from burger and chips, sausage and chips or a jacket potato with beans, cheese and salad.

Children will also receive a drink and an ice lolly; the drinks take the form of cuplets of orange juice. There is no buffet car on the train, so if the adults in your party want anything to eat or drink they will have to purchase it from the buffet at Bitton station, either at the beginning or at the end of the trip.

N.B. There are also vegetarian options available.

How many Children?

Birthday parties are for up to 16, 32 or 64 people (including adults). These specific numbers are due to the sizes of the carriages.

Cost

Avon Valley Railway applies a minimum charge for children's birthday parties, which is £50.00 for up to 32 people and £100.00 for up to 64 people. The total cost of your child's birthday party will depend on the number of people attending and whether or not Avon Valley Railway is providing the catering. It is best to check with the venue for details.

The charges for the journey element of the party vary according to whether the train is being pulled by steam or diesel. There is no charge for the first two adults in any birthday party and the charges for the remaining guests are as follows:

Child Fare: £5.50 by steam or £5.00 by diesel.

Adult Fare: £7.00 by steam or £6.50 by diesel.

N.B. There are specific days for steam journeys and specific days for diesel journeys. You should also note that the above prices do not include catering, which is charged separately per the details in our 'Food' section above.

What's Included?

The venue does not supply party bags, birthday cake, candles or items for cutting and serving the cake. You will therefore have to provide these items yourself if you want to include them in your child's birthday party.

Points to Consider

Avon Valley Railway cannot guarantee that journeys will take place at the stated times, and if alterations to the timetable or the menus need to be made you will not receive any notice. However, the company makes every effort to ensure that trains depart at the stated times where possible.

Chapter 17: Find the Right Chemistry

Science Parties

OVERVIEW

For something a little different, why not try a science party? Not only are science parties a little different but, believe it or not, they're also great fun for children. Additionally, while the children are having fun they're also learning. If your children enjoy learning about science then it could even nurture an interest in what is a valuable subject. Science parties are available in a number of ways. Firstly, if you are lucky enough to have a major science museum located near to you then you could try hosting a party there. Secondly, you could try Mad Science, a company that organises science parties. Lastly, you might want to arrange your own science party. We will take a brief look at each of these options in turn.

Museums are not the boring, stuffy places that they used to be during my childhood. Nowadays they are more interactive, and science museums in particular have many hands on activities that children can take part in. Our case study features the Science Museum in London, which hosts children's birthday parties involving an IMAX 3D cinema experience. The museum has plans for other birthday parties in 2014, with the following themes: Spaces Parties, Flight Parties and a customisable option. A budget option is also being considered. The Science Museum in London isn't the only one that hosts children's birthday parties, as parties are also available at the Museum of Science and Industry (MOSI) in Manchester. You can find more information through the website: www. mosi.org.uk. If there is a science museum located near to your home, it is worthwhile enquiring whether it hosts birthday parties.

Another option for birthday parties is Mad Science at www.madscience. org. The company has franchises located around the world and its aim is to teach children about science in a fun way. As well as children's birthday parties the company runs various programmes, workshops and special events. During birthday parties children can take part in fascinating science demonstrations and activities with the aid of a 'mad scientist'. You can host the party at a venue of your choice because the party organisers will come to you, and they cover many regions in the UK. There is a map on the website to enable you to find your nearest branch of Mad Science.

If you prefer to host your own science themed children's party then you could check out Sizzling Science at: www.sizzlingscience.co.uk. The company sells science related toys and equipment for children through its website. You can also buy party bags and other printed material for science based birthday parties. If you opt to host your own children's science party, then bear in mind that you will have to keep the children occupied with fun games and experiments related to science. You will also have to ensure that you use child friendly products and that none of the equipment is dangerous. Furthermore, you will need to organise the venue and catering.

CASE STUDY
The Science Museum at: http://www.sciencemuseum.org.uk/.

Tel: 020 7942 4460 for party bookings (9.30am – 5.00pm Monday to Friday).

Email: info@sciencemuseum.ac.uk for general enquires, but for party bookings it is best to telephone the party booking line.

The Location
The Science Museum, Exhibition Road, South Kensington, SW7 2DD.

Preparation

You can reserve a child's birthday party by contacting the booking line and paying a £50.00 deposit. It is best to book as soon as possible as there are only two time slots a day in the restaurant for birthday parties. These are at specific times, which are 11.00am and 4.00pm, and they soon get booked up, particularly those that are at the weekend. Generally most parents tend to book birthday parties at the Science Museum six to eight weeks in advance. It is possible to book a party at short notice e.g. a week, but this would be subject to an available birthday party slot in the restaurant. Additionally, you would have to pay in full straightaway.

For the party to go ahead you must confirm no later than two weeks before the date of the party; at this point you will also have to pay the balance. A point worth noting is that the Science Museum does not take birthday party bookings for school holiday periods during February half-term, October half-term, Christmas and Easter. However, it is possible to book weekday parties during the summer holiday period.

The Science Museum provides a free, downloadable birthday party invitation template on its website. This invitation lists the activities that children will be taking part in during the birthday party. These include: watching a film at the IMAX 3D cinema, having lunch, visiting a special exhibition, having a ride on the motion simulator, visiting the Science Museum galleries and visiting the interactive Launchpad gallery. This is useful as it gives parents an idea of how long the party is likely to last.

Some of the activities listed on the birthday invitations are free and some are charged. The film and lunch are included in the Big Screen Birthday package as detailed below. Visits to special exhibitions and the Science Museum galleries including Launchpad are all free once you are inside the museum. However, if you want the guests to have a ride in Red Arrows or Legends, there will be an additional charge. N.B. If you visit other areas of the museum you will be responsible for supervision of the children; the Science Museum Birthday Co-ordinator is not responsible for accompanying you to these areas.

If the number of children attending the party is less than the number you specified when making the booking, you will have to give 48 hours' notice in order to receive a refund. On the other hand, if more children turn up, the Science Museum will try to accommodate your requirements. You will need to speak to your Birthday Co-ordinator at the beginning of the party.

The Party

On the day of the party you will be met by your Birthday Co-ordinator who will help you to store your coats and bags, and will then escort you from area to area, making sure that you are on time for the film. He or she will also make suggestions for things to do and let you know which activities are taking place. If you have included a ride in your party package, your Birthday Co-ordinator will arrange for you to jump the queue, and will collect you after each activity.

Your birthday party can include a range of attractions as described above. However, you will not be able to book exclusive use of the Science Museum, which is a major attraction and has huge numbers of visitors every day.

Big Screen Birthday

There is a standard birthday package called the 'Big Screen Birthday'. This package consists of a meal at the Deep Blue Café and watching a film at the Science Museum's IMAX 3D cinema, and usually lasts between two and two and a half hours. The children will spend 45 to 50 minutes watching the film and an hour in the Deep Blue Diner plus some time meeting up and walking around the museum. As the restaurant has waitress service, the staff will take care of serving the food and clearing up after the children have eaten.

Children will be captivated by the IMAX 3D cinema experience, which uses digital surround sound. The enormous screen is taller than four double-decker buses and fills your peripheral vision. This means that children will feel as though they are a part of the on-screen action, enabling them to experience exciting events such as the weightlessness of space or diving to the bottom of the sea. N.B. IMAX is not recommended for children less than five years of age, and all under 12s must be accompanied by an adult.

The Science Museum allocates a Birthday Co-ordinator for the party who will be on hand to organise the party and answer any questions. The Birthday Co-ordinator will process your tickets and escort you around the various areas of the museum, ensuring that you arrive on time for each booked event. However, none of the museum staff are responsible for supervision of the children, so you will have to look after them as they make their way around the museum. You should try to ensure that there is one adult for every four children attending the party in order to ensure adequate supervision. The charge for the Birthday Co-ordinator is mandatory and is included in the booking fee.

Other Party Options

At the time of producing this guide, the Science Museum staff are looking at a number of other options for birthday party packages, which involve activities other than the cinema visit. These should be available in early 2014, and details are as follows:

- *Space Party* – This includes a ride in Legends of Apollo, a 20 minute activity revolving around the subject of space, and a party meal.
- *Flight Party* – involving a ride in Red Arrows, a 20 minute activity revolving around the subject of flight, and a party meal.
- *A Budget Option* – This will consist of a film, drink and popcorn, and will be priced lower than the other options.
- *A Customisable Option* – Details have not yet been finalised but this option would enable parents to select their own rides and activities.

As part of these proposed new party options, the Science Museum staff are working on a trail for the Space and Flight galleries. This is a form of challenge based in these particular areas of the museum. Children would have to complete the trail, and the first to complete it would win a prize. The trail will either form the basis for a party on its own, or parents will be able to select it as an add-on to other party activities.

Suitable Ages

Children have to be at least five years of age to attend parties with the Science Museum due to the suitability of the party activities. Most children that attend parties at the Science Museum are aged between seven and nine, but occasionally parents will request parties for children slightly younger or older than this age group.

Food

Children's party meals are served in the Deep Blue Café within the Science Museum. Children have a choice of main courses together with a dessert and a choice of drinks, as follows:

- *Main Course*

Children can choose from the following:

- Fish finger sandwich
- Cheeseburger with chips
- Cheese, bacon and potato bake
- Penne bolognese
- Penne with tomato and basil sauce

– *Dessert*

A scoop of ice cream. Children can choose from either vanilla, chocolate or strawberry flavour.

– *Drink*

Children can choose from milk, apple juice, orange juice or tap water, which are included with the price of the party. If children want any other drinks from the menu, these are charged separately.

You are advised to order meals in advance if possible as this speeds things up, especially if you have a large party. However, if you want to order any extra items on the day, or the adults want to order anything to eat or drink, you can do so. You can also ask the café staff to add the additional items to your bill. Please note that the Science Museum cannot guarantee that there will be no trace of nuts in the meals.

How many Children?

Science Museum parties are for groups of at least 10 children. The restaurant allocates 30 seats per booking. As parents are required to have 1 adult attending the party for every 4 to 5 children that means that there would be sufficient seating for around 25 children. On occasions the birthday party staff at the museum can ask the restaurant to increase the numbers slightly, but the maximum overall number permitted is unlikely to exceed 35.

Cost

Prices for birthday parties are as follows:

– *Big Screen Birthday* (as described above) - £12.00 per child.

N.B. There is also a one off booking fee of £50.00 per birthday party, which covers the administration costs plus the provision of a Birthday Co-ordinator.

You can also choose from a number of optional extras, as follows:

– *Red Arrows Ride* – at a discounted rate of £4.00 per child or £5.00 per adult.

– *A Ride in Legends* – at a discounted rate of £4.00 per child or £5.00 per adult.

– *Birthday Cake* – Double chocolate fudge cake which allows for up to 20 portions. The chef uses natural ingredients and cakes are individually made to order, on site - £30.00 per cake.

– *Party Bags* – Party bags contain party bubbles, a pattern maker, Magic Wigglees drawing kit, and a small puffa ball - £5.95 per party bag.

What's Included?

Big Screen Birthday parties include:

- Free, downloadable birthday party invitations
- A meal and drinks at the Deep Blue Café as detailed above
- A 45 to 50 minute film at the IMAX 3D cinema
- The services of a Birthday Co-ordinator
- A visit to any of the other free exhibitions that are taking place in the museum

There are also a range of optional extras that can be added to your child's birthday party. These are detailed in our 'Cost' section above. N.B. The other parties that we have described in the 'Party' section are new future additions so it is best to check the website for up-to-date details.

Points to Consider

If you prefer to bring your own birthday cake, you can do so, and the restaurant will provide you with the appropriate cutlery and a knife to cut the cake. Don't forget to bring some serviettes to wrap the individual portions for the children. There are also a number of points that you need to consider, as follows:

1) The party area in the café will only be available during your party meal and cannot be reserved for the entire duration of the birthday party.

2) Due to health and safety, and fire regulations you are not allowed to take candles (for the cake), balloons or party poppers into the Deep Blue Café.

3) The museum doesn't have its own specific parking facilities for the public. However, pay and display parking is available outside the museum, as well as NPC car parks that are only about three or four blocks away from the museum. Imperial College, which is situated nearby, also has some parking available for the public, but there is a charge for this.

Chapter 18: Keep them Dancing for Joy

Dance Parties

© Dance Mania Parties

OVERVIEW

Dance parties are a fabulous way for children to have fun and burn up some of their boundless energy. There are a number of companies that will organise children's dance parties for you. We have chosen Dance Mania for our case study, which hosts children's dance parties in Essex and the surrounding counties. Although Dance Mania parties are not available throughout the whole of the UK, we have featured their parties because the company offers such a comprehensive package. They will organise the whole party for you from start to finish including venue hire, dancing, party games and the catering if you require. However, their service is customisable so you can choose to include as many services as you wish.

For people who don't live near to Essex, there are other companies that organise children's dance birthday parties. Two examples are Active-Creative (www.active-creative.com) and Diddi Dance (www.diddidance. com). Active-Creative organise a range of children's dance parties targeted at different age groups and they travel to your chosen venue. The company is run on a franchise basis so the children's parties are available in various parts of the UK. It is best to check with the company to find out about availability in your area. Diddi Dance is aimed specifically at preschool children. Again the company is run as a franchise and the party planners come to a venue of your choice. Through the contacts page of the website you can find out which areas of the country are covered. The contacts page also lists the contact details for each franchisee, and gives a link to further information about the person who looks after the parties for each region.

To find other dance party organisers you can either enter 'children's dance parties (+ *your location*)' in an Internet search engine or try the search facility at http://www.whatson4kidsparties.co.uk/.

Many parents may prefer to host their own children's dance party, and the good thing about this type of party is that they are easier than most to organise yourself. You just need to arrange a venue, catering and music. The venue could be your home if there aren't too many children and you have room for them to dance around. To ensure that the children are kept occupied, it may be a good idea to organise dance-related games or general party games rather than just switching on the music and expecting them to respond. You may also consider hiring a venue, which could be a church hall, community centre or hotel function room. There are many DJs that are used to playing at children's parties so you could ask around. You may even find one that will organise games to keep the children entertained.

If you are organising your own children's dance party then you need to make sure that it is age appropriate and that it will appeal to your child's friends. If the children are too young, they may require more structured activities to keep them occupied. Alternatively, if they are too old then they may have outgrown this type of party. If your child is enjoying discos organised by school or youth clubs then that is a good gauge as to whether he or she may enjoy a dance party. It's obviously best to check with your child first though.

CASE STUDY

Dance Mania Parties at: http://www.dancemaniaparties.co.uk.
Tel: 0773 800 1080.
Email: dancemaniaparties@hotmail.co.uk.

The Location

Dance Mania studios are situated at: 26 High St, Billericay, Essex, CM12 9BQ, and some of the children's birthday parties take place there. However, Dance Mania operates throughout Essex and nearby surrounding counties. The staff use different venues in the vicinity, which are hand-picked to ensure they are of a high standard and have all the necessary amenities for a successful child's birthday party.

Preparation

It is advisable to book as far in advance as possible. A good time frame of about three months in advance is recommended, although some bookings are made as far ahead as nine months, whereas other bookings are made only two weeks beforehand. You can book your child's birthday party either by phone or email using the above contact details. In order to secure your booking you will need to pay a deposit and, once you have done so, you will receive your party invitations which are included with all bookings. If you want Dance Mania to arrange the catering for you then they will need sufficient notice, and it's also a good idea to let the staff know in advance if you will require any optional extras such as food for adults.

The Party

Dance Mania is run by a professional performing arts teacher, Jo d'Unienville, who is the primary host for children's birthday parties. There are other staff involved who all work closely with parents to help them arrange a birthday party which can be personalised to suit your child's wishes. Parties usually last for an hour and a half but it is possible to arrange longer parties if required.

The difference between Dance Mania and a lot of other companies that offer dance-themed birthday parties is that Dance Mania have a more comprehensive service than most. They source and hire the venue as well as decorating it, include games and prizes along with dancing, and have a selection of optional extras to make your child's birthday party really special. They have even teamed up with a catering company and a confectioners to enable them to provide high quality party food and party bags. You can see full details of what is included in our section below.

Many of the birthday parties are held at the Dance Mania dance studios in Billericay, and you will have exclusive use of the studios for the duration of the party. If you prefer to have your party elsewhere, Dance Mania will source the venue for you. The company hosts birthday parties across the whole of Essex, and also in Hertfordshire, Cambridge and other surrounding areas.

Apart from the birthday child's parents, none of the other parents have to stay on site as Dance Mania takes care of everything. Your party host Jo always has assistants that work with her at the parties. For most parties Dance Mania will provide two members of staff (Jo plus an assistant) but for parties of 25 or more Jo will be accompanied by two assistants. The Dance Mania party package includes food, and the staff clear up after parties. However, they also offer an entertainment only option, which does not include organising the event and food. With this option you would make your own arrangements for the venue and catering as well as clearing up after the party.

All Dance Mania staff have experience of working with children and are trained in first aid. The business also has CRB checks in place and is gradually increasing the level of training for staff so that they will eventually be trained in health and safety procedures as well.

Suitable Ages

Parties are for children from 3 to10 years of age, and all games, dance and food are varied to suit the age group attending the party.

Food

You have the option of providing your own catering or letting Dance Mania arrange it for you. Dance Mania food is buffet style and includes the following:

- Sandwiches with fillings of ham, jam, cheese and chocolate spread
- Sausage rolls
- Cocktail sausages
- Pizza
- Chicken goujons
- Vegetable platter with dip
- Crisps
- Popcorn
- Fresh fruit platter
- Homemade cupcakes

N.B. For the cupcakes you can choose from a selection of designs, styles and flavours.

If parents choose to stay at the party and would like something to eat, Dance Mania can also arrange the catering for adults. This will take the form of a buffet, and Dance Mania also offers a hot drinks package as an optional extra, which is detailed in our 'What's Included?' section below.

How many Children?

The recommended guideline numbers are a minimum of 15 children and a maximum of 30. However, Dance Mania can host parties for as few as 10 children and as many as 40, so it is best to discuss your requirements with the staff.

Cost

There are various price bands for the parties depending on what you want to include but the starting price is £155.00 for a party that lasts one and a half hours or £190.00 for a party that last two hours. Parties at these prices do not include catering, but they do include the following:

- Party entertainment with a specially choreographed dance routine and a game of pass the parcel
- Decoration of the party area with banners, bunting and two helium balloon displays
- Sweets for the children to take away

N.B. Full details of the entertainment and all other items included as standard are given in our 'What's Included' section, below.

Dance Mania also has several options that include food as described in our 'Food' section above as well as other items. These parties are priced on a per child basis, and details are as follows:

- *£13.95 per child party package* – all of the above plus the venue hire, and a helium balloon for each child to take home.
- *£15.95 per child party package* – all of the above plus party cones filled with sweets (an alternative to party bags).
- *£18.95 per child party package* – all of the above plus the hire of a face painter or a glitter tattooist.

You can add the hire of a face painter or glitter tattooist to any of the other packages at a cost of £60.00 upwards, depending on the number of children attending the party and the distance travelled. Additionally, Dance Mania offers a hot drinks package for adults at a cost of £25.00 upwards. Lastly, you also have the option of adding a candy buffet to any of the party packages at a cost of £80.00 - £90.00 upwards.

What's Included?

All birthday parties include the following as standard:

- Birthday party invitations
- Venue hire and decoration
- Disco ball lights
- A short, choreographed dance routine which is taught to the children during the party and performed to the parents at the end
- Party games with prizes
- Bubble machine fun

There are also a number of optional extras. We have given the prices for these in our 'Cost' section above, and the items are as follows:

- Party food as described above
- Face painting and glitter tattoos
- Helium balloons
- Party bags/cones

If you would also like Dance Mania to provide a birthday cake, these can be sourced from a company that makes bespoke cakes at a price of £40.00 upwards.

Points to Consider

Parents normally take their own serviettes, candles and matches for the birthday cake as well as a knife to cut it. However, if you do happen to forget any items, the Dance Mania staff always carry spares.

One point worth bearing in mind is that Dance Mania staff pride themselves on tailoring every party to your exact specifications. Therefore, they will ask you for details of your child's favourite songs so that they can generate a customised playlist for use at the party. Similarly, if there are any games that your child and friends are particularly fond of, you should let the Dance Mania staff know so that they can include them on the day. In addition, if you are planning a particular theme, inform the staff and they will incorporate it with the party. This includes colour schemes, or the types of designs or toppings that you would like for the homemade cupcakes. You should also let the staff know if any of the children have allergies or special dietary requirements.

Chapter 19: Go out for Dinner

Restaurants and Cafés

OVERVIEW

In recent years there has been an explosion of restaurants targeted at kids, and the good thing is that most of them are relatively inexpensive. Although many of them sell fast food (and you may not therefore want your children to dine there regularly), a birthday party is a special occasion so it's a good excuse to indulge.

Some of the particular restaurants that offer children's birthday parties are Pizza Hut, Pizza Express and McDonald's. Pizza Hut features a 'Make your own Pizza Party' which is great fun for children. The parties include many extras such as party bags and invitations. You can find out more about them on the Pizza Hut website at: www.pizzahut.co.uk/restaurants by visiting the 'Kids & Families' section. Pizza Express also offer a 'Kids' Pizza Making Party' including a side salad and dough balls. There is a parties section of the website with more information at: http://www.pizzaexpress.com/parties.

We have featured McDonald's in our case study because its restaurants are widespread throughout the UK, and prices are reasonable. Of course there are many other child-friendly restaurants that also have branches throughout the UK. Therefore, you should have no problem finding a local restaurant where you can host your child's party.

Our case study features parties predominantly aimed at children aged between five and nine although it is possible to hold parties there for children of other ages. As children get older, however, they enjoy going out for meals with a group of friends (as opposed to their families) to celebrate special occasions. The age at which children choose to do this varies but generally this refers to teenagers. Initially, they will want parents to drop them off at a restaurant then pick them up after the meal, until they are old enough to share taxis. They will normally be in their late teens before they reach the stage where they are making their own way to and from a restaurant using public transport.

Restaurants that are popular amongst teenagers include Frankie and Benny's (www.frankieandbennys.com) and the World Red Hot Buffet (www.redhot-worldbuffet.com), but you may find others. Frankie and Benny's is an American 1950s style restaurant serving Italian food. There are more than 200 branches in the UK and the restaurants allow you to take your own birthday cake. The staff will then present the cake during the meal and lead the party guests in singing Happy Birthday.

The Red Hot World Buffet, as the name suggests, is a buffet style restaurant popular with adults as well as children. They serve dishes from various countries and customers can eat as much as they like at specific sittings. Although the Red Hot World Buffet doesn't host birthday parties as such, the 'all you can eat' basis appeals to teenagers who have big appetites, and the restaurants do accept group bookings. There are currently only seven branches of the Red Hot World Buffet in the UK, but they have proved so popular that the company is expanding rapidly.

CASE STUDY

McDonald's Restaurants at: www.mcdonalds.co.uk.
Tel: 08705 244622 for McDonald's Customer Services or fill in the online contact form on the 'Contact Us' page of the website.

N.B. To find the contact details for your local McDonald's restaurant you can use the online Restaurant Locator.

The Location

McDonald's has more than 1,200 restaurants in the UK. Customers can use the Restaurant Locator tool on the McDonald's website to find their nearest restaurant and see which restaurants host birthday parties and have a Play Place.

Preparation

Parents looking to book a birthday party at McDonald's should contact the manager of their local restaurant to enquire.

Once a birthday party is booked you will receive a booking confirmation, 15 invitations and a food order sheet to help you pre-organise the children's party meals. The 15 invitations will usually be given at the point of booking, or you can pick them up nearer to the date of the party. Each individual restaurant usually decides how far in advance they will accept bookings, so you will need to enquire with your nearest McDonald's that offers birthday parties.

Restaurants may ask for a deposit, depending on how busy their schedules are.

The Party

For their birthday party at McDonald's children can choose between a Jungle theme or an Ocean theme, and the parties usually last for around an hour and a half to two hours. The party will be held in a specially reserved area of the restaurant and there will be a fully trained party host to run the party and keep the kids entertained.

The Jungle adventure story lets kids embark on an imaginary journey deep into the jungle in search of the lost city and its hidden treasures. Kids can choose which animal they want to become from a selection of cheeky face masks.

The Ocean adventure story takes kids on an imaginary journey across choppy seas to venture beneath the ocean waves in search of lost treasure. Kids can become pirates or mermaids on their quest for the hidden treasure.

When you and the children arrive at the party you will need to ask for the party host, who will take the children's food order. The children will all be issued with stickers to enable the party host to identify which children are part of the birthday party and who the birthday child is. Once everyone has arrived the party will begin. The party host will encourage the children to play fun, themed games accompanied by music and using themed floor mats.

The party food arrives in a special box and each of the children will also receive a party bag which the parents can pre-fill with goodies. The birthday child receives a special adventure pack as a present.

Each of the party hosts are specially trained and will have attended a training course which covers:

- Booking a party
- Preparing a party
- Hosting a party
- Health and safety
- Face painting

Parents can stay at the party if they want to, or use the time to grab a coffee and have a catch up. There does, however, need to be at least one parent in the restaurant at all times for every five children present, in order to assist with supervision. An additional adult must be present for every child that is five years old or under.

The party structure usually involves playing games for about 60 minutes, then eating lunch or tea followed by one more game at the end of the party. However, this is a suggested guideline for the parties, which may vary slightly from restaurant to restaurant. Although parties usually last between one and a half and two hours, parents and children are welcome to stay as long as they like.

Generally there is one host that is dedicated to the party. However, depending on the size of the group, two hosts may be required. Restaurant staff are usually responsible for clearing the tables after a party is over, but parents are responsible for looking after the children's belongings and presents.

Suitable Ages
The themed parties at McDonald's are aimed at children between 5 and 9 years of age. The party host can assess the age group and tailor the party to suit different ages if necessary.

Food
Currently, every child will be able to choose from one of the following:

- Hamburger
- Cheeseburger
- Four Chicken McNuggets®
- Three fish fingers

Accompanied by one of the following:

- Small portion of fries
- Carrot sticks
- Fruit bag

Children can also choose from a large selection of drinks including:

- Robinson's Fruit Shoot®
- Organic milk
- Buxton ® mineral water (still)
- Tropicana® orange juice
- Milkshake
- Small Fruitizz (made with fruit juice concentrates of grape, apple, raspberry and lemon mixed with sparkling water)
- Cola
- Fizzy orange

How many Children?

The maximum capacity for birthday parties depends on the venue being used and can be discussed with the restaurant manager when booking. However, standard McDonald's party kits (which are issued to restaurants) include 15 of each item. Larger groups can often be accommodated if sufficient notice is given.

Cost

McDonald's Birthday Parties start from £5.99 per child, but it is important to note that prices may vary between restaurants.

McDonald's can supply a birthday cake as an optional extra. You can ask for more details when booking your party with the restaurant.

What's Included?

All children attending a McDonald's Birthday party will receive a McDonald's Happy Meal and elements of the McDonald's Party Kit. Each individual Party Kit contains enough stock for a party of 15 children, and the contents are:

- 1 food booking sheet
- 15 placemats (Jungle or Ocean themed)
- 15 napkins
- 15 Happy Meal boxes
- 15 balloons (helium or normal, Jungle or Ocean themed)

- 1 sticker sheet (to identify the kids at the party)
- 15 adventure passports and reward stickers (Jungle or Ocean themed)
- 15 jungle animal masks (Jungle party kits only)
- 8 mermaid wands and crowns and eight pirate hooks and hats (Ocean party kits only)
- 15 straw attachments (Jungle or Ocean themed)
- 15 party bags (Jungle or Ocean themed - kids can put their passports in them and parents can pre-fill them with goodies)
- 15 activity books (Jungle or Ocean themed)
- 1 birthday child gift book and envelope (Jungle or Ocean themed)

N.B. Many of the restaurants also offer face painting.

At the end of the party the birthday child will receive a special adventure themed activity book.

Points to Consider

The birthday cake offered by McDonald's is a chocolate cake. Some restaurants offer their own birthday cakes but this is dependent on the individual branch of McDonald's. The restaurants can supply candles, which are usually incorporated into the cost of the cake. If you choose to bring your own birthday cake you would also have to bring your own candles. Generally, most parents prefer to bring their own cake to fit in with their party theme.

A small number of McDonald's restaurants have parking restrictions in the restaurant car parks. Where these apply they will be clearly signposted. Therefore, if you or any other adults attending a McDonald's birthday party are likely to stay in the car park for longer than the allowed time limit, you should make yourselves and your car registration number known to the restaurant manager on arrival. This enables the restaurant staff to make special parking arrangements for you.

Chapter 20: Hit the Shops

Shops and Stores

OVERVIEW

Children's parties based in shopping centres and stores are already popular in the US and are a growing trend in the UK. These types of parties can take on many forms depending on the particular shops, so we'll start by looking at our case study. This features birthday parties that are held at the Trafford Centre Creche and Play Area.

The Trafford Centre is enormous and has an entertainment complex built in. However, apart from the Trafford Centre, there are other major shopping centres in the UK with similar facilities. In fact, the Trafford Centre is part of the Intu group, which looks after 12 large shopping centres including Lakeside in Essex and the Metrocentre in Gateshead. You can find the other centres through the Intu website at http://intu. co.uk. This will enable you to check whether there is one near you offering children's parties. Intu is not necessarily the only company whose shopping centres host children's parties though, so it's worthwhile checking out others that are located close to where you live.

As well as children' parties held in major shopping centres, some stores host their own in-store parties. Good ones to look out for are those hosted by the Build-a-Bear Workshop, and Ikea. With the Build-a-Bear parties children get the chance to make their own cuddly toy. Although there are extras included with the parties, such as photos, thank you cards and a free virtual party room at bearville.com, Build-a-Bear does not include catering. However, as their shops are often located in major shopping areas, you may find it possible to feed the children elsewhere. Ikea stores usually have restaurants and some of them have crèches that host children's parties. So, if you have an Ikea store near to your home you might want to check whether they have these facilities.

Another store worth mentioning is Hamleys, the famous toy shop, which has branches in London, Glasgow, Dublin and Cardiff. Although you would probably have to live near a Hamleys store to make this a viable option, they offer a great selection of parties. You can choose from a Hamleys Tour to a really special Sleepover Party with lots of fun party options in between. There are also a range of add-ons that you can select with most of the parties. Options vary depending on the branch and prices differ accordingly. You can find more details by going to the party page links of Hamleys' website (www.hamleys.com), which you can find at the bottom of the home page screen.

CASE STUDY

The Trafford Centre Creche and Play Area at:
http://intu.co.uk/traffordcentre/centre-information.
Tel: 0161 746 9000.
Email: ttclcreche@btconnect.com.

The Location

Creche and Play Area, Unit 1B, The Orient, The Trafford Centre, Manchester, M17 8AA.

Preparation

Birthday parties at the Trafford Centre Creche and Play Area need to be booked at least two weeks in advance, and you will need to pay a deposit of £15.00 when you make your booking. The deposit is non-refundable in the event of cancellation, but staff at the venue will try to find you an alternative date for your child's birthday party.

There are three different birthday party packages available, which are classed as Bronze, Silver and Gold. The Silver and Gold packages include invitations but these are not included with the Bronze package. However, for Bronze parties you can purchase the invitations separately.

If you book a party that includes invitations, you will receive them as soon as you pay the deposit.

With the Silver and Gold packages you will need to pay the balance of the total party cost at least three days before the date of the party. For Bronze parties, on the other hand, the balance of payment is not required until the date of the party. You will also need to give the venue details of your food choices for Silver and Gold packages when you pay the balance. This will give the staff sufficient time to order the party food.

The Party

All parties last for two hours, which consists of time spent in the play area and time spent eating and drinking. Apart from eating the meal, the birthday cake will also be presented while the children sing Happy Birthday. Parents are welcome to involve the children in additional games if they want to. For Silver and Gold parties the children will spend roughly 90 minutes playing and 30 minutes eating and drinking.

The play area has a range of equipment for children including a large ball pool, tube crawls, slides, climbing nets and rope swings. There is also a dedicated Little Tikes play area for children under six years of age. Children will have their party food after the play session and they are not allowed back into the play area once they have eaten. Details of the three party packages are:

- **Bronze Package** – The Bronze package does not include food, but it includes 90 minutes in the play area and use of the party room. For Bronze parties you would usually arrange your own catering for the party.

- **Silver Package** – The Silver package includes 90 minutes in the play area and use of the party room. Food is also included per the section below as well as invitations, placemats and party hats.

- **Gold Package** – The Gold package includes everything that comes with the Silver package plus party bags and a birthday cake. In addition, all children attending the party receive a voucher for 50p off their next visit to the creche and play area, and the birthday child receives vouchers for two free visits.

For all parties you will need to ensure that you have sufficient adults to supervise the children as this is not the responsibility of the staff at the venue. The venue requires a ratio of one adult to every eight children, with a minimum of three adults for every birthday party. However, you will need to ensure that there are more adults if children are under three years of age, as each child under three will need to be accompanied on the equipment at all times. You also need to ensure that children are supervised when using the lift.

The venue supplies one member of staff to help organise the party and the staff clear up the dining area after the party has finished. Additionally, the Trafford Centre Creche and Play Area ensures that there is always somebody available who is trained in first aid.

Suitable Ages
The play equipment is designed for children from the ages of 3 to10. Children under 3 years of age can attend birthday parties but they must be accompanied by an adult. The Trafford Centre Creche and Play Area also has a height restriction of 5ft.

Food
For the Bronze package you would have to organise your own catering. However, for the Silver and Gold packages food is delivered to the Party Room. The food for the Silver and Gold parties is supplied by either Harry Ramsden's, Burger King or the Greenery from their children's menus, depending on the choices that you have selected. These restaurants are all located close to the venue.

There is no food available for adults at the Trafford Centre Creche and Play Area. The venue is situated in an area of the Trafford Centre which has a range of restaurants, but if you wanted to eat during your child's birthday party you would have to ensure that sufficient adults stayed with the children to supervise them.

How many Children?
All birthday parties are for a minimum of 8 children with a maximum of 40, providing there is sufficient space available.

Cost
The prices for each type of party are as follows:

- *Bronze Package* - £5.00 per child and £5.50 during weekends, school holidays and bank holidays.

Party bags are available as an optional extra at £1.00 per child, and invitations are also available at a cost of £1.00 for 10.

- *Silver Package* - £8.50 per child and £9.00 during weekends, school holidays and bank holidays.

Invitations are included with the Silver package per the details above, and party bags are available as an optional extra at £1.00 per child.

- *Gold Package* - £11.50 per child and £12.00 during weekends, school holidays and bank holidays.

Invitations and party bags are included with the Gold package as well as a number of other items, which are detailed above.

What's Included?

Full details of the three party packages, and the items included in each, are given in the above section headed 'The Party'.

Points to Consider

If any of the adults bring pushchairs for their children, these must be folded and stored in the reception area. To lock your pushchair up you will need to pay a £1.00 refundable deposit. The play area has its own toilets, which are equipped with baby changing facilities.

The venue will provide a knife to cut the cake and napkins to wrap it in, and you are requested not to bring your own knife to the party. You are also not allowed to bring helium balloons, hot drinks or re-lightable candles. With Bronze and Silver packages you will need to provide your own birthday cake and candles but these are both included with the Gold package.

Chapter 21:
Go Green

Garden Centres

OVERVIEW

A children's party at a garden centre may not be an obvious choice but it can be a novel and fun way for the children to enjoy themselves. Many garden centres nowadays are large and sophisticated. As well as being a good place to buy anything garden related, these larger centres also have various retail outlets, aquatic centres, pet sales, and a restaurant. In fact, some of them have so many shops and attractions that they make a great family day out.

A good example of this is the Klondyke Garden Centre group (www.klondyke.co.uk), which has more than 20 separate centres in various parts of Scotland, Wales, the North West and the North East of England. Their Brookside Centre in Poynton, Cheshire, for instance, has various plants for sale, an aquatic centre, gift shop, clothing shop, craft shop, pottery shop, model shop and restaurant. It also offers children's parties and has a miniature railway offering family rides around the centre, which are particularly popular with children.

Another example is the Garden Centre Group (www.thegardencentregroup.co.uk), which hosts children's parties in the restaurants at 50 of its garden centres. The participating centres are widely spread throughout the UK, and the parties consist of a hot, set menu with a choice of main courses, a sweet and drink, or a cold buffet, plus time spent in the play area.

Frosts Garden Centres (www.frostsgardencentres.co.uk) also offer children's parties with a choice of six different party themes. The parties are available through their centres at Milton Keynes, Bedfordshire and Oxfordshire.

We have chosen Dobbies Garden Centres for our case study as these are sophisticated centres with many shops and attractions. They are widespread throughout the UK and the majority of them have high standard restaurants offering children's parties. Children have a good choice of party food and the party activities are stimulating and engaging.

Children's parties do not just take place in the larger garden centre groups, of course. There are many regional garden centres, with only one or two branches, that may offer children's parties. You can find out what is available in your area by searching the Internet for 'garden centre children's parties (+ *your area*)'.

CASE STUDY
Dobbies Garden Centres at: http://www.dobbies.com/.
Email: customer.service@dobbies.com.
Tel: 0131 561 6406.

N.B. These are the contact details for the head office, but you would have to contact your local Dobbies restaurant to book a birthday party per the details in our section headed 'Preparation'.

The Location
Dobbies has 34 garden centres in England, Scotland and Northern Ireland. Each of the garden centres has a restaurant and various shops. You can find your nearest store by selecting the 'Our stores' tab from the website menu.

Preparation
It is advisable to book your children's birthday party with Dobbies as far in advance as possible. You will have to pay a £5.00 deposit when you make the booking. Each Dobbies restaurant will have different availability for parties in terms of dates and times. It is therefore best to contact the restaurant manager to enquire about availability. You can easily find the phone number of each branch of Dobbies via the website. Just select 'Our stores' on the menu, then click on your chosen store to the left of the page. Store details will then show up together with the telephone number on a panel at the bottom right of the page. You will need to ring this number and ask for the restaurant manager.

Dobbies does not provide birthday party invitations so you will have to take care of these. You will also need to let Dobbies have the children's party food choices in advance of the party date.

The Party

Dobbies are very sophisticated garden centres; as well as selling gardening products they have various shops at each centre and a restaurant. Many of the shops are food related with an emphasis on fresh, local produce. This therefore means that parents could spend time wandering round the shops whilst the children enjoy the party. Alternatively, you could choose to have something to eat and drink in the restaurant. You should ensure, however, that sufficient adults remain at the party in order to supervise the children. The required ratio is one adult to every five children.

Children's birthday parties last two hours and take place inside Dobbies' restaurants, which are bright and spacious areas located inside each Dobbies Garden Centre. For the duration of the party you will have exclusive use of a room, or section of a room, which will be specially decorated. The birthday child will receive a Little Seedlings themed gift. N.B. the Dobbies Little Seedlings Club is a free gardening club for children aged between four and 10 years of age. It teaches them all about plants, wildlife and the Environment. You can find out more about the Little Seedlings Club by visiting the Dobbies website.

A personalised birthday cake is also included in the cost of the party. Children can choose from a selection of hot and cold meals. They will usually have their party meal before taking part in a choice of restaurant-based activities, as follows:

Cressy Caterpillars

The children will mix cress seeds with compost then fill a nylon pop sock with the mixture. They will secure the ends of the sock using elastic bands and use two further large elastic bands to tie around the sock in order to divide it into three equal parts. They will then stick antennas and sticky eyes at one end of the sock to form the caterpillar's head.

The children take their creations home and are instructed to keep them moist. When the cress seeds start to grow and come through the sock, it resembles a caterpillar shape made of cress.

Cupcake Decorating

Children will use ready-made cupcakes which they will then decorate, using various toppings to make their cake as colourful as possible. At the end of the party they can take their cupcakes home.

Pizza Making

Under the guidance of Dobbies staff, children can use a range of toppings to design their own pizza, which is then cooked in the oven by Dobbies chefs. Once the pizzas are cooked the children can eat them at the party.

N.B. Pizza making is only available at these locations: Milngavie, Melville, Lisburn, Aberdeen, Braehead, Livingston, Carlisle, Ashford, Peterborough, Liverpool, Gillingham, Inverness and King's Lynn.

Dobbies supply sufficient staff to cover parties according to the number of children attending and they will clear up after the party. However, it is not their job to supervise children, which is why you need to ensure that sufficient adults stay at the party in order to take care of the children.

All Dobbies staff are specifically trained according to their role. This applies in particular to the staff that work in the restaurants. When Dobbies hold in-store events, such as children's birthday parties, the store team completes a risk assessment. This ensures that the health and safety procedures will be sufficient for the event, and highlights any areas where extra measures have to be put in place in order to add an extra level of protection. Additionally, all Dobbies stores have a minimum of two fully trained first aiders available at any point throughout the day.

Suitable Ages

There is no minimum age requirement for children attending Dobbies parties but the maximum requirement is 14 years of age.

Food

Children can choose from a hot or cold meal. The cold meal takes the form of a packed lunch and includes the following:

- A sandwich
- Cheese
- Yoghurt
- Fruit
- Jelly
- Capri Sun

For the hot meal children can choose from the following:

- Sausage and chips
- Macaroni cheese
- Fish goujons and chips
- Chicken nuggets and chips

Children can opt for vegetables instead of chips if they prefer and each of the hot meals comes with jelly and a Capri Sun.

How many Children?

The minimum and maximum numbers of children that can attend parties will depend on the capacity of the individual Dobbies restaurant and can range from between 10 and 50. It is therefore best to check with the restaurant manager at your chosen Dobbies Garden Centre.

Cost

Dobbies birthday parties cost £9.95 per child. Please refer to the following section for details of what is included in this cost.

What's Included?

Dobbies children's birthday parties include the following:

- Exclusive use of a room or area of the restaurant which is decorated for the party
- A personalised birthday cake
- A 'Little Seedlings' themed gift for the birthday child
- A choice of hot or cold party food – full details in our 'Food' section
- A choice of birthday party activities as described above

Points to Consider

As well as including the birthday cake in the cost of the birthday party, Dobbies provides candles for the cake. Dobbies staff will also present the cake and divide it into individual portions for the children.

If parents want to make additional arrangements for their children's parties they are welcome to do so. This could involve, for example, party balloons, further decorations or hiring a clown.

Chapter 22: Zap the Opposition

Laser Tag and Paintball

OVERVIEW

Laser tag and paintball are usually aimed at older children, particularly paintball, which is also played by adults. As the name suggests, paintball uses gelatine balls that are filled with paint, and these are fired at opponents using a special paintball gun. The ball explodes on impact covering the target in coloured paint, so it's easy to tell if an opponent has been hit. Because the paint splatters when the ball explodes, the game can get messy. Getting hit by a paintball can be slightly painful too depending on how far the paintball has travelled. Many paintball operators provide protective clothing or advise you to wear old clothes because they will get dirty.

Paintball can be held either indoors or outdoors at venues that are specifically designed for the game. Some will have bunkers or objects that players can hide behind. Players are usually part of a team which plays against another team. Typical games involve trying to capture the other team's flag whilst preventing them from capturing your flag. Most paintball venues cater for young adults and often attract stag and hen parties. However, it is possible to find venues that allow older children to play. A company called UK Paintball has special Junior Days and you can find out more through the website at: http://www.ukpaintball.co.uk/. However, if your child is under 18 years of age you will have to sign a disclaimer on their behalf before they will be allowed to play. UK Paintball has more than 60 venues throughout the UK.

Laser tag has a lower minimum age requirement than paintball, although it is still unsuitable for very young children. The minimum age requirement for the organisation featured in our case study is seven years of age. Unlike paintball, laser tag does not involve contact with any form of missile, such as a paintball. Players use a gun which fires a laser beam at the opponents. As all players wear a vest, contact with the target is recorded electronically, and this is known as a 'tag'.

The objective of the game is to tag opponents as frequently as possible whilst avoiding being tagged yourself. As with paintball, venues are specially designed and the sport can be played indoors or outdoors depending on the facilities at the particular venue. Indoor games are usually played in a dark arena full of ramps, strip lights and theatrical fog to create atmosphere. Because the arenas are dark inside this could be frightening for younger children. Another point to note is that if you object to your child playing any kind of gun-related games then both of these sports are best avoided. Having said that, laser guns are completely harmless in the physical sense.

There are several companies offering laser tag in the UK. Our featured organisation, Laser Quest, has 26 venues. If there isn't a Laser Quest arena near you then you may want to try Sector 7 as it also hosts children's parties. It is connected with Tenpin (http://www.tenpin.co.uk/), which we have featured in an earlier chapter, and laser tag is available at various venues. Details can be found on the website under the 'Activities' section.

You may also want to try Operation Laser Tag (www.operationlasertag.co.uk), which offers mini laser tag sessions for children from six to nine years of age using mini laser guns. The games take place in an outdoor arena and children wear lightweight taggers instead of the usual vests, which can be quite heavy. Operation Laser Tag has venues at Yorkshire, Wakefield and Rochdale. The organisation also offers extras for children's parties, which consist of party bags and a party meal of pizza and a drink.

CASE STUDY

Laser Quest has 26 arenas in England, Ireland, Northern Ireland and Scotland, and each of the venues has a separate website. However, you can locate each of the websites by going to the 'Locate' page of the main Laser Quest website. Apart from the arenas, Laser Quest is also involved in the manufacture and supply of laser tag equipment. Founded in 1988, it is now the biggest laser tag operator in the world and is continually researching and developing new equipment.

We have based our case study on Laser Quest at Blackpool to give an example of what is involved in a typical laser tag party, so we have also given the contact details for Blackpool below. The birthday packages differ slightly at each venue depending on the facilities available. Furthermore, as each arena is run independently, the prices will also vary slightly, so it is best to check your nearest venue for specific details.

Laser Quest: http://www.laserquest.co.uk/.
Tel: 01625 586 647 or 07919 173641.

Laser Quest, Blackpool: http://www.lqblackpool.co.uk/.
Tel: 01253 620056.

Alternatively you can book through the Blackpool Laser Quest website using the online booking form.

The Location

This case study is based on the Blackpool venue which is situated at: 66-74 The Promenade, Blackpool, Lancashire, FY1 1HB. Please check the Laser Quest main website for other venues.

Preparation

Advance booking is essential for all birthday parties. You can book your party online for the Blackpool venue (and many others) using the booking form on the website for that branch. Alternatively, you can ring the Blackpool venue on the above telephone number. Invitations are supplied by the venue and can be downloaded from the website when you make your booking. Laser Quest staff recommend that you book at least six weeks in advance. This will give you a good chance of securing your chosen date and time. A 50% deposit is required when you make your booking and the remaining balance is due on the day of the party. Guests are asked to arrive 15 minutes before the party is due to start.

The Party

All of the parties at the Blackpool venue include two games of laser tag and last for one hour and forty five minutes in total. At the end of the second game the children will spend 30 minutes eating and drinking in a private party area where a party host will be on hand to help. Laser Quest, Blackpool supplies at least one member of staff for up to 10 players. For parties with more than 10 players, two members of staff are supplied. There will always be at least one member of staff available who is trained in first aid. Each of the guests attending the party will receive a themed Laser Quest party bag and the birthday child will receive a gift voucher.

For laser tag, the children taking part are fitted with body packs and a laser gun, which they use to stalk opponents and zap them. All equipment is provided and staff brief the children on how to use the equipment. The laser beams are not harmful and children do not feel anything when they are struck by a laser. Sophisticated equipment records each hit so that players earn points each time they zap an opponent but lose points if they are zapped. The Laser Quest arena is very atmospheric with mazes, catwalks, swirling fog, lights and music. At the end of the game the scores are displayed on a monitor and each child taking part will receive his or her own score card.

Parties can be booked Monday to Friday, or weekends, but different prices apply for weekends, school holidays and bank holidays. All prices are detailed in our 'Cost' section below.

There are two different types of parties. One is the Party Adventure where the party guests share use of the Laser Quest Arena with members of the public; the other type is an Exclusive Party Adventure where guests have exclusive use of the arena. The second type of party works out more expensive, with a one off fee applicable rather than a cost per child.

Suitable Ages

Children must be at least 7 years of age to take part in laser tag at the Blackpool venue. There will be a minimum age requirement for all laser tag venues so it is best to check.

Food

Food is supplied by Burger King so children have a choice of Burger King kids' meals. They will also be provided with an unlimited amount of orange or blackcurrant squash during the meal.

How many Children?

The minimum number of children that can attend any birthday party is 8 and the maximum is 20.

Cost

Charges for each type of party are as follows:

- *Party Adventure* - £12.95 per child Monday to Friday and £14.95 per child for parties at weekends, school holidays, and bank holidays.

- *Exclusive Party Adventure* – a set fee of £240.00 no matter when the party takes place.

What's Included?

All of the birthday parties include:

- Free downloadable party invitations
- Two games of laser tag
- A themed Laser Quest party bag for each of the guests, which contains an alien toy, badges and various sweets and chocolate
- A gift voucher for the birthday child
- A choice of Burger King kids' meals for each child
- Unlimited orange or blackcurrant squash for each child
- 30 minutes spent in the party zone area after laser tag has taken place
- The assistance of a party host

Points to Consider

Laser Quest do not supply birthday cakes so it is best to bring your own together with candles. However, Laser Quest will provide everything else that you need including cups, napkins, a knife to cut the cake and a lighter for the candles.

You will need to ensure that the party guests are aware of the rules of play as they contain important safety information about Laser Quest.

Chapter 23: Have a Great Day Out

Tourist Attractions

Image supplied by Alton Towers

OVERVIEW

There so many fabulous family attractions in the UK, and although I have already covered farms and zoos in previous chapters, I felt that due to the huge volume of tourist attractions, this merited a separate chapter. Additionally, many of these attractions offer children's parties. Here is a list of some of the attractions that offer party packages:

- Chessington World of Adventure
- LEGOLAND
- The London Eye
- Madame Tussauds
- Sea Life Centres
- Sea Life Sanctuaries
- Blackpool Tower
- The Dungeons, London
- Thorpe Park
- Warwick Castle

You can find more details on the Merlin Groups website at: http://www.merlingroups.co.uk/friends-family/birthdays/. N.B. the parties apply to adults too, so it is best to check what is on offer for children in particular.

The advantage with having a party at a child oriented tourist attraction is that the entertainment is already at hand. This means that, in many cases, children can spend the entire day exploring the attraction as well as attending the birthday party. You will have to check with the individual attraction for their arrangements though, as this may incur an additional fee. With Alton Towers, for example, which is featured in our case study, the party takes place in the waterpark but you can get a group discount if the children want to visit the theme park.

We have chosen Alton Towers for our case study because it is a popular attraction and offers a choice of parties that are designed to appeal to children. Also, it is a theme park so it is typical of the type of attraction that is child centric. As well as entertainment, Alton Towers children's parties include a buffet style meal and several other extras.

Of course, Merlin Groups do not have the only tourist attractions in the UK and you may find it possible to locate others in your area. You could search the Tourist Information Centres website at: www.touristinformationcentres.com to find attractions near to you, and then check whether the attractions host children's parties.

CASE STUDY

Alton Towers Resort at: http://www.altontowers.com/.

Tel: 0871 222 3330 for birthday party bookings.

The Location

Alton, Staffordshire, ST10 4DB.

Preparation

You should use the above telephone number to make your birthday party booking, which should preferably be made at least a week before the party. The venue does not take a deposit but prefers you to pay in full at the time of booking. If this is not possible, then you will need to make payment in full no later than 10 days before the party. When ringing Alton Towers to place a booking, you will need to provide the following information:

- Your name, address and postcode
- Your email address
- The date and time of your child's party
- The age that your child will be on his/her birthday
- The total number of children that will be attending the party
- The total number of adults that will be attending the party

If your chosen date and time is not available, Alton Towers will let you have a note of other dates and times that may suit you. N.B. There is no need to give food orders in advance as the food is served buffet style, so the children can choose what they want to eat during the party.

Party invitations are supplied by Alton Towers and can be downloaded from the website. There are height restrictions, so it is best to make other parents aware of this when you send out invitations. Children under 1.1m tall cannot use the Master Blaster slide. However, they may use Rush 'N' Rampage if they are under 1.1m tall but over 3 years old, provided they sit on a parent's knee. There are no height restrictions on Flash Floods slides.

You will also need to ensure that all children under 10 years of age are adequately supervised at the party. There should be one responsible adult for every child under five years of age and one adult for every two children aged between five and nine. The term 'adult' refers to anyone aged 16 and over.

The Party

There are three types of birthday parties specifically for children at Alton Towers, which are the waterpark birthday party, the golf birthday party and the combined waterpark and golf birthday party. Parents can join in either of these parties, but they will have to pay Alton Towers' standard charges for their chosen activities. These charges are published on the website. All of Alton Towers' staff are trained in health and safety including those that help out at the birthday parties.

If your child and his friends prefer to visit the theme park rides you can receive a discount for group party bookings. Details are given below in our cost section. N.B. This option is not an organised birthday party so you would have to make your own arrangements regarding food and supervision of the children.

Waterpark Birthday Parties

Birthday parties take place in the lagoon-style waterpark and last for two hours. Alton Towers operates a 'queue busting' system for the birthday child during the party, which enables faster entry for some of the busier rides. Children eat their party meal in the Splash Landings Hotel which has fabulous themed surroundings. This is a comprehensive party package and full details are given below in our 'What's Included?' section.

Extraordinary Golf Birthday Parties

This party centres around the nine-hole 'Extraordinary Golf' course and lasts for as long as it takes the children to go round the golf course, plus the time allocated to eating their party food afterwards. The golf course has a range of obstacles based on some of the Alton Towers' rides and attractions, which the children work their way around whilst playing golf. The golfer with the best score wins a prize. Food is served in the themed surroundings of the Splash Landings Hotel. Again, the party is quite comprehensive and full details of what is included are given in our section below.

Combined Waterpark and Golf Birthday Parties

For an additional charge of £4.00 per child you can have a combined waterpark and golf party, which will include all the features from both types of party.

Suitable Ages

There is no minimum age requirement for children's birthday parties, but the maximum age is 16.

Food

The party food is served buffet style in Flambo's restaurant overlooking the Caribbean Waterpark. Children will be able to choose from a variety of dishes from around the world. If parents want to eat, they can order a buffet meal separately on the day of the birthday party.

How many Children?

The minimum number of children required for a birthday party booking is 8. There is a maximum limit of 25 people attending each of the types of birthday party. The latter number includes adults.

Cost

- ***Waterpark Birthday Parties*** - £14.95 per child.
- ***Extraordinary Golf Birthday Parties*** - £14.95 per child.
- ***Combined Waterpark and Golf Birthday Parties*** - £18.95 per child.

N.B. There is a charge of £10.00 each for adults attending the party. This includes a two hours swim and party food in Flambo's.

Group Discounts for Theme Park Entrance

- For groups of between seven and nine children there is a 30% reduction on the usual price.
- For groups of 10 or more there is a 35% reduction on the usual price.

N.B. To qualify for these discounts you will need to book in advance via the website.

What's Included?

- ***Waterpark Birthday Parties***

All waterpark birthday parties include:

- Party invitations which can be downloaded from the Alton Towers website
- Two hours spent in the waterpark
- A 'queue busting ring' for the birthday child to use on Calypso Creek, Rush 'n' Rampage, and Master Blaster
- A birthday party meal for each child served in Splash Landings Hotel
- A party bag and balloon for each child
- A birthday card for the birthday child

- ***Extraordinary Golf Birthday Parties***

All golf birthday parties include:

- Invitations which can be downloaded from the Alton Towers website
- A round of golf on a nine-hole crazy golf course
- A special prize for the child with the best golf score
- A birthday party meal served in Splash Landings Hotel
- A party bag and balloon for each child
- A birthday card for the birthday child

Points to Consider

Alton Towers allows photography inside the waterpark but not inside the changing rooms. There is no video recording allowed anywhere in the waterpark.

You can either bring your own birthday cake for your child's party, or Alton Towers Resort will provide one at a cost of £15.00.

Alton Towers ask that you give special attention to the following:

- – Let the venue know if any of the children have special dietary needs.
- – Be aware of any strong or weak swimmers in your party.
- – Take a note of the supervision of children ratios.

N.B. You can find further details of all these requirements on the Alton Towers website at: www.altontowers.com.

Find out More about My Books

Further copies of "Great Places for Kids' Parties (UK)" are available to purchase through Amazon in a digital version or a print version. You can also find out about my other books through my Amazon author page at: http://www.amazon.co.uk/Diane-Mannion/e/B008MX8LD0. Print copies of the book will also be available through other stockists. You can find more details on the books page of my website at: http://www.dianemannion.co.uk/books.html.

About the Author

Diane Mannion started her writing career 14 years ago when, whilst studying towards her writing diploma, she began to work as a freelance writer, publishing many articles in well-known UK magazines. These included a series of parenting articles for the former 'Mum's Survival Guide' section of Bella magazine. Through contacts she then had the opportunity to work with a web developer, as well as producing a series of case studies for Manchester Education Department regarding parental involvement in their children's school life.

As a result of these two opportunities Diane began to put her writing skills to use in other areas. She developed a knowledge and understanding of copywriting techniques and SEO copywriting through attending various courses combined with practical experience.

Since 2007 Diane has operated Diane Mannion Writing Services, a business offering a range of copywriting, editing and proofreading services to businesses and individuals. Diane employs other trusted and skilled freelancers on an ad-hoc basis to help with larger projects.

One of the areas where Diane has gained a great depth of expertise over the years is in ghost writing books on behalf of clients. This is an area of the business that Diane finds particularly rewarding because of the sense of achievement in having completed a lengthy piece of work.

This is the second parenting book written by Diane Mannion, which combines her talents in book writing together with experience both as a parent of two teenagers and as a writer of parenting topics. We hope you find this book useful.

You can find out more about Diane Mannion Writing Services at: www.dianemannion.co.uk, or by emailing: dianewriting@googlemail.com. You can also follow Diane on Twitter: @dydywriter, and on Facebook at: www.facebook.com/DianeMannionWritingServices.

Also by Diane Mannion

Non-Fiction

Kids' Clubs and Organizations – A Comprehensive UK Guide

It's a growing dilemma for parents in these recession hit times:

- Spend a fortune keeping the kids entertained;

- Or have them screeching round the house driving you to despair?

But what if there was an inexpensive alternative?

'Kids' Clubs and Organizations' introduces you to literally thousands of groups that provide kids' activities and events at little or no cost to families. You'd be surprised at the number of children's pastimes that you never even thought about.

Clubs and organizations are available for all age groups from babies to young adults, providing a broad range of enriching and educational experiences. Although the book is aimed primarily at UK parents, there are plenty of useful ideas for all parents.

By enrolling your children into a local club or organization you can:

- Prevent your children from becoming bored and disruptive
- Give yourself a break and a chance to wind down
- Discover talents that you didn't know your children had
- Meet other parents in a similar situation
- Help your children develop new skills
- Take pride in your children's achievements
- Help your children to make new friends
- Get the satisfaction of seeing your children happily engaged in worthwhile activities

For ease of use I have divided the book into 24 chapters with each one focusing on a particular kind of group. I start the chapters by giving an overview of the type of club or organization. Further sections then give details of: 'Who can join?', 'Benefits', 'Costs', and 'How to Find a Group'. I have devoted the last section of each chapter to those parents who may want to get involved themselves. In some instances you can even start your own group.

'Kids' Clubs and Organizations' is the first book of its type in the UK giving a definitive guide to the wealth of groups that are devoted to children. Sometimes it's just a matter of knowing where to find the right group and that's where this book can help.

Although each chapter gives specific information for each type of club or organization, I have also included general sources of further information in the last chapter.

Find out More - To find out up-to-date news about where to buy the book please refer to my website at: http://www.dianemannion.co.uk/books. html. You can also find updates on the Diane Mannion Amazon author page at: http://www.amazon.co.uk/Diane-Mannion/e/B008MX8LD0, on my Twitter feed at: @dydywriter and on my Facebook page at: www. facebook.com/DianeMannionWritingServices.

Fiction

My first novel is scheduled for release in early 2014:

Slur

Julie Quinley is a young woman with everything to live for – a good job, a loving family, an active social life and a doting boyfriend, Vinny. Unfortunately, however, the dramatic events of one fateful night are about to change the course of her existence forever.

When one of Julie's workmates dies of a drink and drugs overdose, Julie and her best friend Rita are wrongly accused of the killing. Julie has to bear the slights and accusations of her office colleagues and life becomes unbearable. The pressure seeps through to her personal life, and, believing that she has lost the respect of her close family and friends, Julie sinks into a pit of despair. Unknown to Julie, however, they are rallying to her support.

Julie reaches a turning point when Rita reveals that Vinny has found out who the killer really is. Realising that she must act in order to clear her name, Julie joins Vinny and Rita in trying to find evidence against their suspect.

Proving a vicious murderer guilty, however, is never going to be easy, especially when the police remain convinced that Julie and Rita are the culprits. After several daring but thwarted attempts at entrapping their suspect, Julie and her friends hire a private detective. Eventually they find the evidence they need and await the trial.

But is he really the killer? A shock discovery in court adds a final twist to the story.

This crime thriller is enriched by a strong interplay of characters throughout. The girls have very colourful personalities and the electrifying atmosphere surrounding them is fully brought to life.

Find out More - A digital version of this book will be available soon. Please view the website: http://www.dianemannion.co.uk/books.html for news of release dates. You can also visit the Diane Mannion Amazon author page at: http://www.amazon.co.uk/Diane-Mannion/e/B008MX8LD0, or find updates on my Twitter feed at: @dydywriter and on my Facebook page at: www.facebook.com/DianeMannionWritingServices.

Disclaimer

The information contained in this book results from extensive research carried out by the author and does not in any way represent an endorsement of any of the services offered by the organisations named in the book. All prices and other facts are based on information obtained through research, and were correct at the time of compilation. However, it is possible that some of the information or websites referred to in this book may have changed since the book was compiled. The author accepts no responsibility for any dealings that you may have with any of the named organisations or with other organisations that provide children's birthday parties.

Special Offers

Silver Blades Ice Rinks
Birthday child goes free
Tel: 08700 852929 and quote the code.
Code: BK01
Expiry Date: 31st December 2014
Offer applies to all branches

Powerleague
Free party upgrade to include a Coach
Code: PL356x9t9i
Expiry Date: 30th April 2014
Offer applies to all branches

The Creation Station
Include a third activity for half price
(worth around £30)
Code: BK02
Expiry Date: 31st December 2014
Offer applies to all branches

The Creation Station
Free upgrade from a Cool Party to a Brilliant Party
Code: BK03
Expiry Date: 31st December 2014
Offer applies to all branches

Make Scents Ltd

One free party place for every 15 children

Code: BK04

Expiry Date: 31st December 2014

Offer applies to a catering party package

Kiddy Cook

Free Kiddy Cook apron for the birthday child

Code: BK05

Expiry Date: 30th June 2014

Offer applies to all branches

My Pamper Parties

10% discount on all parties

Code: BK06

Expiry Date: 30th June 2014

Offer applies to all branches

Chill Factor^e

10% discount on weekend parties

Tel: 0843 596 2233 and quote the code

Code: Birthday10

Parties must be booked on or before 31/10/15 and taken on or before 31/3/16

Chill Factor^e

20% discount on parties held Monday to Friday

Tel: 0843 596 2233 and quote the code

Code: Birthday20

Parties must be booked on or before 31/10/15 and taken on or before 31/3/16

Warwickshire Country Parks

£8 discount on birthday parties

Code: BK07

Offer applies to bookings made between 1st April 2014 and 30th June 2014.

Dance Mania Parties

10% discount on all parties

Code: DMP10

Expiry Date: 31st December 2014

Trafford Centre Creche and Play Area

Birthday child goes free for parties with over 15 children

Code: BK08

Expiry Date: 30/12/14

Laser Quest, Blackpool
Birthday child goes free
Code: BK09
Expiry Date: 31/12/14
Offer applies to the Blackpool venue only

It is best to note that organisations will have their own stipulations relating to special offers. For example, some may reserve the right to withdraw or amend promotions without advance warning. If in doubt it is best to check with the company directly to find out more.

1. To qualify for our Special Offers you will have to quote the relevant code and provide proof of purchase for this book.
2. For the Creation Station, both offers can be used together.
3. The Chill Factor[e] offers are subject to availability and cannot be used in conjunction with any other offer or promotion.

Notes

FRCS General Surgery
Viva Topics and Revision Notes